1st In-Line

1st In-Line

Roll up to get ahead with this street-wise instruction
manual on In-Line Skating

Mark Heeley

NEW
BURLINGTON
BOOKS

A QUINTET BOOK

Published by New Burlington
Books
6 Blundell Street
London N7 9BH

ISBN 1-86155-076-6

This book was designed and
produced by
Quintet Publishing Limited
6 Blundell Street
London N7 9BH

Creative Director: Richard Dewing
Art Director: Patrick Carpenter
Design: Roger Fawcett-Tang
Senior Editor: Anna Briffa
Editor: Lydia Darbyshire
Photographer: Jeremy Thomas
Illustrator: Jim Bamber and
Linda Millard
Demonstrators: BladeMarc and
Samantha Tusson Ford

Typeset in Great Britain by
Central Southern Typesetters,
Eastbourne

Manufactured in Singapore by
Eray Scan Pte Ltd

Printed in Singapore by
Star Standard (Pte) Ltd

Publisher's note
The author, publishers, and all
those involved in the compilation
of this book cannot accept any
responsibility for injury or damage
arising from in-line skating. In-line
skating is potentially dangerous,
and all skaters should wear full
protective gear at all times.
Although some of the skaters
shown in this book are not
wearing this equipment, in-line
skaters should wear wrist guards,
knee and elbow pads, and a
helmet while participating in the
sport. Skate smart, skate safe.

To Maggie
From the unforgettable moment
in Boston, it was an unforgettable
year. Thank you. Thanks also
to Boston, San Francisco, Vail,
New York – and, of course, all
our friends.

Contents

New wheels. New bo
A whole new way to

dies. New minds.

travel on planet earth

01   Introduction

Pedestrians stop and gaze in bewilderment; those in traffic look on with curiosity; most stare in fascination and delight. Some will even wave you down, quizzing you while they take a closer look.

You bid them farewell, stretching into a stride then a glide. Silently you pass trees, bushes, and buildings. The wind rushes by; your eyes water, your heart pounds, the adrenaline pumps. With lengthening strides, you accelerate, legs and arms synchronized as each dynamic movement sends wheels spinning and the world speeding by.

Speed, power, control: gradually fun becomes excitement, excitement becomes exhilaration. It is like nothing you've experienced before. This is IN-LINE SKATING: a sport, a recreation, a lifestyle.

Easier than ice skating and skiing, in-line skating is like going for a run on wheels, but without the pounding, the monotony, and the discomfort. Physical exertion is forgotten, being replaced by enjoyment in the satisfaction of mastering and controlling velocity. This is a whole new way to travel on planet earth.

Experience the great excitement of achieving maximum speed, power, and control. Photograph courtesy K2.

*Perfect synchro-
nization of arms
and
legs makes for
more dynamic
movement.*
Photograph cour-
tesy K2.

In-line skating's best-known bike path along LA's Venice Beach.
Photograph: Stockfile/ Steven Behr.

Where there is asphalt, you'll find in-line skaters: from Los Angeles to Chicago, Minneapolis to Manhattan. And what began in the USA has spread around the world: London, Paris, Munich, Rome, Barcelona, Amsterdam, Toronto, Tokyo, Sydney, and many other places. It is as if someone has opened the doors of an ice-skating rink and said, "Go on, keep going!"

In-line skating can be practiced for a wide variety of reasons: for fitness, transportation, hockey, extreme cross-training, or just plain, simple fun. Because of this diversity, it achieves much exposure on TV and in magazines and newspapers. As a result, in-line skating has reached the top of the charts in new-generation sports.

Because there are so many ways to participate in in-line skating, it appeals to many different people. It is a truly international sport that attracts all ages, from 6 to 60, and both sexes from a variety of cultures.

For many, the term "skating" is unsuitable for this new-found passion. Instead, "blading" or "rollerblading" is commonly used. These terms have been adopted from the skate brand "Rollerblade®," the manufacturers of which have been credited with creating the first commercial in-line skates. However, in an attempt to protect its valuable trademark, the Rollerblade® company is campaigning vigorously against the generic use of its brand in this way.

Skates for the whole family – in-line skating appeals to all ages.
Photograph: Stockfile/Steven Behr.

Pausing to
quench a thirst
after some
serious skating.
Photograph
© *Jack Gescheidt.*

Time Warp

The first in-line skates were developed by a Dutchman in the 1700s in an attempt to simulate ice skating in the summer. Over two centuries later, in 1980, two American brothers from Minneapolis established a factory to manufacture the first ever in-line skates on a large scale, under the brand name "Rollerblade®." Originally, the skates were sold to ice-hockey players as an off-season training aid, but the brothers soon realized that people were also using their skates for recreational purposes. From then on they broadened their horizons and promoted their wares to a much wider audience. By 1988, in-line skating had captured the imagination of over a million Americans, and by 1993 it had spread around the world; there are as many as 25 million people skating today.

Unlike "quad" roller-skating, in-line skating is faster and more dynamic; the sensation is more like being on ice skates or skis. The reason for this is wheel dynamics. A quad skate has outer and inner wheels, and when cornering, the inner wheels travel a shorter distance than the outer wheels. This makes high-speed turning or skating on uneven surfaces unstable and inconsistent. With in-line skates, however, turning is precise and accurate, because the wheels follow the same arc.

Hockey can be one of in-line skating's most exciting applications. Photograph courtesy Rollerblade®

Home is in the half-pipe for the aggressive in-line skater.
Photograph
© Jack Gescheidt.

Skate the World

The following pages will give you an insight into the wide world of in-line skating, and you will learn just about everything you need to know to get you going. You might find yourself dreaming of conquering the extreme to become an aggressive skater, the radical end of the sport where only the half-pipe, ramps, rails, and mean streets can provide enough adventure to stimulate the adrenaline flow. Learn how to perform a Mute Fakey or a grinding toe-slide in the danger zone of in-line skating.

Perhaps you would prefer the social interaction and competitive fun of roller hockey. This rapidly growing sport is probably the quickest way to progress in skating. With stick in hand, you are forced to learn quickly as you weave between players, passing and receiving the puck, reacting to its changing direction and speed in the controlled boundaries of a pitch. Roller or skater hockey has changed rapidly in the last few years, adopting new rules and techniques. Thanks to in-line skates, things have really hotted up.

Dare to air – flying time at NISS Competiton, L.A.
Photograph
© Jack Gescheidt.

Rhythm in two's. Skating with a friend is twice as much fun.
Photograph courtesy K2.

Racing is at the elite, competitive edge of the in-line skating spectrum, and it is the purest representation of sport. It is the most specialized and physically demanding of all the applications, but it offers probably the greatest individual rewards. Speed, strength, and stamina are essential elements of in-line skating's most technically subtle discipline.

The cross-training benefits of in-line skating are enormous. Fitness is a by-product of participation, but skiers, snowboarders, cyclists, mountain bikers, and runners, not to mention ice-hockey players, are among the many athletes who are discovering the enormous benefits that in-line skates can bring to their cross-training programs.

A scene from the IISA 100K World Championships in New York.
Photograph © Jack Gescheidt.

In-line, in-life. Everyone has a need for speed. Photograph: Stockfile/ Steven Behr.

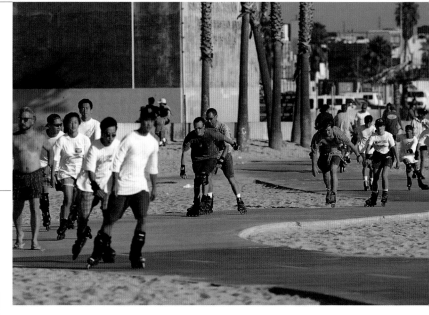

Easy Rolling

So you want to be a part of the action! You don't have to be a sportsperson to share the enjoyment of in-line skating: if you can walk, you can skate. This book will show you how to progress easily and safely, using clear, step-by-step photography accompanied by simple, instructional text. There are no secrets to learning the techniques; you will find this book works with you, motivating and stimulating, identifying common mistakes, and offering you corrective techniques to keep you on-line in-line.

Use the information as you want. The photographs will give you 80 percent of the information you need to progress to the next maneuver; the text will back up what you see.

If you want to progress in in-line skating, there can be no substitute for actual practice. However, this book will provide the best and quickest route to the pleasures this exhilarating sport has to offer. Enjoy each step along the way, and before you know it you will be speeding along bike paths, sidewalks, and streets, reaching new heights and discovering new thrills.

Cool breezers. Take life easy in the skate lane. Photograph: Stockfile/ Steven Behr.

How to Use This Book

➜ Read the introduction to each move to get an overview of why, how, and what you will be doing.

➜ Check the symbols opposite so that you know the primary techniques required to perform the new move.

➜ Look at the photographs to get a visual impression of what is required.

➜ Look at the photographs again, this time reading the captions so that you know what you should be doing.

➜ Learn the step-by-step routine. Once you have learned how to complete the maneuver, you will be able to ignore the numbered, sequential moves, because the overall movement will be automatic.

➜ Read the explanations that accompany each move so that you fully understand it.

➜ Use the skate-tracing diagrams to help you understand the path your skate and wheels should take.

➜ If you have problems, look at the Troubles section at the end of each chapter.

Stroking

V-walking easily becomes stroking. If you have practiced this on grass, you will not have experienced the sensation of rolling, but you will, ideally, have an understanding of what is required to perform this relatively easy technique. Stroking is really a slower form of striding, the technique that you are working toward.

Until you understand what you are doing, the most effective way to learn is to follow set patterns. At first, these might seem very mechanical, but as you practice, you will repeat the patterns often enough that they will become automatic. To make it easy, the techniques have been described as three-step routines, which break down the maneuvers into digestible chunks, and to simplify other techniques, three-step routines will be used throughout

the book. Once you have adopted the maneuvers naturally and they become automatic and flowing, you will be able to discard the sequence routine.

From the Ready Position, begin to V-walk, with your weight forward. When you have gained a little momentum, place your skates parallel to each other and then begin a routine of propelling yourself forward by scooting one skate at a time. The difference this time is that, by tilting the skate and pushing it gently out to the side, you will produce more energy and, therefore, more significant forward motion. Make one stroke at a time with each leg, bringing the skates back parallel to each other and into a moving Ready Position. This will give you time to check your balance between each scoot, preparing you for the next stroke.

1 From the Ready Position, begin to V-walk to gain some momentum, keeping your weight forward.

2 Stay on the inner edges of the wheels and scoot the skate out sideways. Make sure the skate goes to the side and not backward, behind you.

Between each stroke you should experience your first taste of gliding. Enjoy this sensation, even though it is slow: it is one of the sensations that in-line skaters live for! The sequence for the V-walk is:

1 **Ready**
2 **Stroke**
3 **Regroup**

Practice stroking and develop a feel for balance on the move. Again, stroking is really only a building block. It will help develop your confidence and take you toward real skating, where stroking and gliding combine to become striding. Once you've had a taste of a little speed, you might be tempted to move on swiftly and get a little more wind in your hair... but, it is a good idea to learn how to stop.

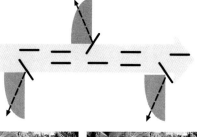

3 *Regroup by bringing the skate back in so that your skates are parallel with each other.*

4 *Your skates must be parallel when you Glide so that you can control your movements at this faster speed.*

5 *Repeat the move with the other leg, then the first, until you have built up a smooth rhythm.*

Key to Symbols

The following symbols appear throughout the text, and accompany the specific techniques that you will learn. By looking at them before you embark on any new technique, you can gain at-a-glance information as to what exactly is involved, and which steps you are likely to need.

Ready Position

V-position

Crossover Technique

Swizzle

A-frame

Dynamic Ready Position

Stroking

Striding

Parallel Turn

T-position

Scissor

Equipment

It is a good idea to rent a pair of skates the first time you try in-line skating. This will be an inexpensive way of deciding if you like it or not.

However, owning your own skates from day one can be a better idea. With a good in-store fitting service, your skates will fit snugly and comfortably, giving you the best possible control and enjoyment so that you progress quickly, whereas an old pair of well-worn rental skates may not be so good. Once you have bought them, your determination will be greater, and let's face it, if you can afford them, there's

Your skates are the most important part of your equipment. Make sure they fit you well, and you'll avoid problems when learning.

nothing like having your own! And don't forget that after paying for five or six rentals, you could have bought your own brand new pair in the first place.

There are several different types of skate on the market, but the most popular fall into the large range of "recreational" skates, which are designed for all-round performance and ease of use, and "fitness" skates, which are generally faster and designed for greater stability at higher speeds. In addition, specialized skates, designed for specific activities, are also widely available. Skates for hockey, racing, and aggressive skating employ materials and features that enable them to perform well in their particular discipline. Each brand offers a different level of performance and, as in most things, you will get what you pay for. Buying cheap skates is not recommended, however, for what you save in expenditure you will lose in performance and, therefore, in enjoyment. If you are buying your first skates, look at those in the mid-price range, but even if you are on a budget, spend as much as you can afford, and think about upgrading later on. Adults should expect to pay $120.00 upward for a good pair of skates; for kids, the quality is less important, but they should still enjoy the benefit of the glide early on, so expect to pay about $60.00 or more.

Comfort is the priority when you are buying skates. Your skates won't feel like slippers, but your feet should be comfortable and there should be no pressure points. Make

Spiritblade LX

Rollerblade Maxxum

sure that the skate is a snug, all-round fit. Your toes must not be pushed right up against the end of the shell, and you should be able to wiggle your toes. Your heel should be held firmly but comfortably, and you should be able to flex your knees and ankles forward. Most good skates are adjustable so that the fit is as perfect as possible. Before you buy, make sure you can adjust them yourself while they are still on your feet.

Before you even try on a skate, however, you must be aware of the gliding potential of your skates. Spin the wheels with your hand; they should move silently and freely. If they grind or stick, the bearings, and probably the wheels too, are likely to be of poor quality, and this is likely to reduce your speed and, therefore, your enjoyment when you try to glide.

In addition to the way the wheels rotate, performance depends on how well the shell flexes and on the quality of the bearings. If you are a first-time buyer, ask the advice of your local supplier, who should be able to suggest the appropriate type of skate for you. In-line skates are available in a wide range of outlets, from traditional skate stores and ski stores, to bicycle and mountain bicycle stores as well as in general sports stores. You'll even find them in some large toy shops. Inevitably, the best skates and the best advice will be found in the specialist retail outlets, where the staff will be specially trained to advise and fit skates. The correct selection and fitting of in-line skates is a serious business, so it is worth seeking out a specialist store.

Buying Skates

➜ Ask for advice on the difference between the brands, models, and styles that are suitable for your level of proficiency and your aspirations. Make sure the assistant understands your needs, and do not allow yourself to be talked into buying the first model the assistant recommends until you have made your needs clear.

➜ Ask about the performance and specifications of the skates, especially the wheels and bearings (see pages 32–34).

➜ Try on at least two – more if possible – styles of skate.

➜ Make sure that the skate fits snugly and comfortably.

➜ Make sure that the model you choose carries a manufacturer's guarantee. Some stores even offer a "comfort" guarantee.

➜ Remember to buy your protective gear at the same time.

➜ Skates below provided by Sun & Snow, Ski 47, and Road Runner.

K2 Extreme Flight

Oxygen KR 1-1

Protective gear should be worn securely all the time.

Protective Gear

The other very important purchase is protective gear, which will protect you against grazing, or more serious injury, if you fall. Do not try to skate without wearing wrist guards, elbow pads, knee pads, helmet pads, and a helmet, all of which are essential for any in-line skater. When you are fully equipped, you will enjoy your skating more, becoming more relaxed and skating with greater confidence. (Protective gear, clothing, and accessories provided by Sun & Snow, Ski 47, and Road Runner.)

Wrist guards

Elbow pads

Helmet

Knee pads

Clothing

Comfort and flexibility are the keys to dressing well for skating. Choose shorts that will protect your hips and thighs – loose-fitting athletic or thick, baggy shorts, for example; or, if you prefer, Lycra® or cyclist's shorts. In cold weather wear sweat pants or leggings.

T-shirts or any kind of non-constricting sports top will do. Cotton will let your skin breath on hot days, and you can easily add a sweatshirt, some fleece or even a wind shell if it turns cold.

Medium weight sports socks or lightweight wool socks are suitable, but even better are the special socks that are made for wearing with skates. Make sure that your socks are smooth and that there are no wrinkles, which could cause blisters.

In-line skating socks are available.

Baggy shorts like these are ideal – even better if they have protective padding.

A cotton T-shirt will help to keep you cool.

Accessories

There is a host of different accessories available for the recreational in-line skater. Some of the accessories available for specialist skaters are described in the appropriate chapters of this book. The best-equipped skaters carry a "fanny pack" or backpack to hold a skate tool for emergency repairs and on-the-spot maintenance. You should also carry a spare brake, wheel, and bearings, a small first aid kit and a whistle. The smartest skaters may want to have their own personal stereos, a portable water-filled back system, cool shades, and a robust watch.

Complete Wheel Systems – in a bottle. Most will contain wheels, bearings, lubricant and more.

Skate carrying kit bags are a must for the traveling skater.

Skater wearing a "fanny pack".
Photograph:
Stockfile/
Steven Behr.

Cool shades are an essential accessory.

Skate mountable torches for night skating.

Components and Maintenance

Wherever and however you skate, you've got to keep you skates in shape. Neglected or badly maintained skates can be unsafe, will perform poorly, and will spoil your enjoyment. Wheels, brakes, and bearings wear, and need regular servicing and occasional replacement. You should also know how to make important upgrades. In fact, knowing how to handle and maintain your skates is as important as knowing how to use them.

In-line skates are relatively simple devices, made up of seven main components. Make sure that you know what these are and where they are located – study the exploded diagram below.

Shell

The shape and design of the shell largely determine the way the skates will perform. Many recreational skates are made of polyurethane polyamide plastics in varying degrees of hardness for varying levels of flex and performance. Other "soft" skates use polymer-reinforced synthetic leather, and in these, for extra comfort, the shell is integrated with the liner of the boot, which is non-removable.

Liner

The degree of comfort will vary depending on the materials used for the liner (inner boot). A thin, badly padded liner or a poorly finished shape will offer only limited comfort, and after a few hours' skating it may distort, causing uncomfortable pressure points. The liners of the best boots are made from durable material and have extra padding.

You can take out the liner from hard shell skates to see how it is made.

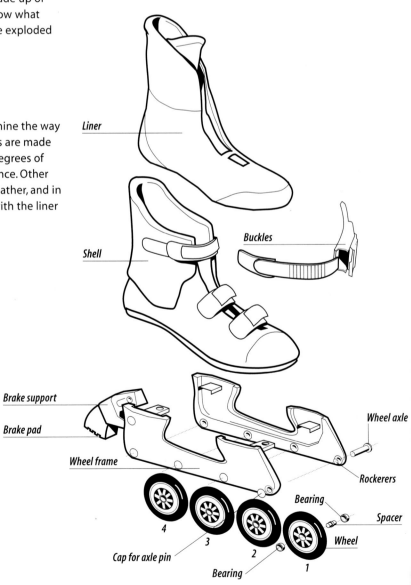

Although a footbed may seem to be an optional extra, it is definitely a wise investment.

Fastenings

Fastening systems vary on skates, but the most commonly used are clips. Some manufacturers still produce laces, which were once the only way to fasten skates, and they are still preferred by some skaters because they offer a closer, more evenly spread fit and, therefore, more precise control. Aggressive, hockey, and racing skaters need laces or something similar to give them additional control.

However, today's clip systems are very sophisticated and can provide enough adjustment for a precise fit. Choose a recreational skate with a multi-clip buckle fastening system for quick, easy fastening. Beware of awkward or difficult fasteners that need several attempts to reach the correct position. Adjustment should be smooth and precise and involve the minimum fuss.

Footbed

The footbed is perhaps the most overlooked, yet one of the most important, features of the skates, especially as regards comfort. Most skates have a standard footbed that provides the foot with adequate support, but footbeds that are made from nothing more than stiff cardboard and that have no soft material under the foot should be avoided. The best type of footbed are custom molded or employ some kind of bio-mechanical technology in their design, and they are usually made by independent companies that specialize in the manufacture of footbeds.

Wheel Frame

The structure that supports the wheels is the frame, which is usually made from glass-reinforced nylon or polycarbonate. The stiffer and lighter the frame, the better the performance. Recreational skate wheel frames cannot usually be upgraded or replaced, but when you buy, check if the frame is "rockerable" (see below). Specialist in-line skaters pay particular attention to the frame, because if affects both control and performance, and, of course, the better quality frames are more durable. Recreational skaters need not be unduly concerned, however.

Rockering for Specialist Performance

When skates come out of the factory, the wheels are un-rockered – that is, they are all level and all in equal contact with the ground for all-round performance. Many wheel frames, however, are designed to allow the wheels to be rockered for tighter, finer turns. When the second and third wheels are positioned lower than the first and fourth wheels, the skate can pivot more easily.

Remove the wheels, prise out the rockerers, and spin them through 180 degrees so that the wheel axle is located higher on the first and fourth wheels and lower on the second and third. If your skate allows you to do this, try rockering the wheels once you have acquired a sufficient degree of skill and you will discover the advantages and disadvantages that rockering can offer.

Bearings

Wheels and Bearings

The wheels and bearings have the greatest influence on the performance of a skate. Learn the internationally recognized grading classifications, and you will be armed with the information you need to reach the right decision when you are choosing a skate. Most new skates are sold with the manufacturer's recommended wheel and bearing package, and in most cases they represent about half the value of the skates. Do not be talked into buying a cheap pair of skates that you think can be upgraded later on – it will only cost more in the long run.

Wheels

Most wheels perform well, but you should avoid cheap, soft wheels that will not roll properly. Wheels are made from urethane plastic, and they range widely in size, hardness, hub type, and profile.

Wheel hardness is measured by durometer. Durometers range from 74A to 100A – the higher the number, the harder the compound. The most popular is 78A, which is hard enough to roll, not too flexible, but soft enough to be comfortable on marginal surfaces.

Wheel size is measured across the diameter in millimeters. The most popular sizes are between 70 and 78 millimeters, and they offer all-round ability and make it easier to cross uneven surfaces smoothly. The larger the wheel, the faster you will be able to roll, especially in a straight line. However, larger wheels give slower acceleration and less scope for turning. Smaller wheels turn more efficiently and allow you to maneuver in tight situations, and they are, therefore, needed for hockey and aggressive skating.

The hub or core of the wheel adds stiffness and rigidity. Racing wheels have large hubs and often have spokes to keep down the weight and possibly help to keep the bearings cool. Hubs get smaller in relation to the size of the wheel to the point at which aggressive wheels do not need to have them.

Bearings

Like wheels, bearings vary widely. But when you are choosing a skate, remember that good bearings spin freely and silently. Poor bearings are easily detectable – the wheels spin noisily and roll with unnecessary drag – and are not very long-lasting. Try to avoid them.

Knowing the specifications of the bearings will help you to predict how they will perform. The internationally recognized standard is ABEC (Annular Bearing Engineering Council), and it is your guarantee that the bearing meets a minimum standard of precision. Bearings range from low-performance, non-ABEC (beginning with Standard, which are the slowest and poorest quality), right through to the fastest bearings, ABEC 5, and even ABEC Pro 5 for elite racing. The gradings are (beginning with the lowest):

Standard	ABEC 1
Semi-precision	ABEC 3
Precision	ABEC 5

When you are buying skates, ask the seller about the bearing specifications. That way, you will get some idea of whether you are going to be able to Glide properly. Look for Precision or ABEC 1 at the very least for enjoyable learning.

Wheels

Allen wrench

Maintenance

Before and after you go skating, get into the habit of checking your skates, making sure that the wheels are secured and rolling freely. Check that the brake still has plenty of rubber and hasn't exceeded its wear limit. Although it is unlikely that your skates will be in a dangerous condition, giving them a safety and performance check is always worthwhile.

Rotating the Wheels

After checking the brake, take a look at the wheels. They will wear more on the inner edges and more rapidly toward the back, where most of your weight will be borne. It is vital that the wheels wear as evenly as possible so that they perform efficiently and safely. Wheels that wear evenly will also last at least three times as long, saving you considerable expense. To achieve an even wear pattern, you need to rotate the wheels.

Rotating wheels means moving their positions – that is, turning them around so that the inner edges are on the outside, as well as moving them from front to back and vice versa. You might have to rotate your wheels every time you go out or only once a month, depending on the surfaces you skate on, and how often and far you go. Normally, you will have to rotate your wheels after about 20 miles of moderate skating, but this is only a guideline – it is up to you to check them regularly.

Use a skate tool or an Allen wrench to unscrew the wheel axles, and withdraw them from the frame to release the wheels, putting the wheel axles and locating bolts or caps in a safe place.

There is a set sequence for rotating wheels, and this is shown in the diagram below.

Swap wheel 1 with 3, and 2 with 4, as well as flipping them through 180 degrees. Because wheel wear is greatest toward the back, don't just inspect the front wheel for side wear – look at all the wheels, especially no. 4 of your lead skate (see page 42), which is prone to the greatest wear. Consider the overall picture of how your wheels wear; they say a lot about how you skate – where your weight is positioned and how aggressively or cautiously you maneuver.

Low-specification wheels, and even good quality-wheels that are exposed to high impacts from jumping or constant bumping, can crack and break. So make sure you inspect them for fractures, and replace them if necessary.

Rotating Wheels

4   3   2   1

Cleaning and Lubricating Bearings

After the wheels, the other components of your skates that need constant attention are the bearings. These do not like sand, water, mud, or grit, and exposure to any of these can clog the bearings, reducing their ability to spin. If they are constantly exposed to these substances, the bearings will seize up and have to be replaced. Water can be particularly deceiving. Always expect that corrosion will occur if you have skated in rain or through puddles.

There are two main types of bearings – serviceable and non-serviceable. The better makes tend to be serviceable, allowing you to take them apart and lubricate them. As soon as you notice any dragging or noise from your spinning wheels, it is likely that the bearings need cleaning and lubricating. Regular bearing maintenance will make them last longer and give better performance.

When you have released the wheels (see Rotating the Wheels, page 33), push out the cased bearings from the wheel and separate them from the spacer. Do this either with the tool that is supplied with the skates or by pressing hard against the lip of the spacer of the wheel to force out the far bearing. Use a finger or a tool to pop out the other bearings. Each wheel has two bearing units, which look like metal donuts, with a spacer between them.

Use a very small flat-head screwdriver and carefully prise off one side of the casing shield, thereby exposing the tiny ball bearings on which so much depends. Discard the shield. Using a light oil or a special bearing lubricant, which will be available from your skate store, clean out all the dirt and grime from the casing and around the ball bearings. The best way to do this is to work on one set of bearings at a time using an old toothbrush and a soft, clean cloth. Remove all the accumulations of dirt, and flush all the components with oil until all traces of grit are completely eradicated. When they are clean, put the ball bearings back into the casing and add a drop or two of oil – do not use too much – and spin the bearing to distribute it evenly.

Replace the bearings and spacers back in the wheels, with the open side facing inward. Put all the pieces back together again, remembering to rotate the wheels if necessary. When you replace the bearings, take care not to over-tighten the axle pin, as this can easily dent the casing and ruin the ball bearings inside.

Now that the bearings are sealed on only one side, dust, water, and grime can find their way back in more easily, so regular cleaning is even more important.

Upgrades

By upgrading the wheels and bearings you will be able to obtain better performance from most skates. Good skates will allow room for larger, better, or specialized performance wheels, while the bearings can be changed as you wish. This means that you can invest less in a pair of skates to begin with, but have the assurance that you are not closing the door to better performance later. However, if you expect to progress quickly and are, therefore, likely to want to make an early upgrade, it is probably worth investing in a better pair of skates in the first place. This is particularly true when you consider that a new set of wheels and bearings can amount to the difference in cost between one pair of skates and another. It is always a good idea to buy the best you can afford within your budget.

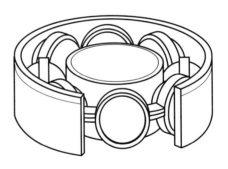

Prize off the outer casing to reveal the working ball bearings inside.

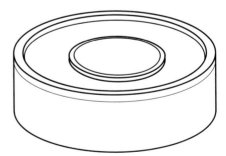

Easy Stretching

A basic level of fitness is necessary for all sports, and although the level needed for in-line skating is probably less than many other types of physical activity, it is important that you do not do yourself permanent harm by over-straining. Take a little time to get your body into shape so that you enjoy skating to the full. After just a few hours' exercise a week you will notice improvements to your body's toning and stamina.

The particular muscle groups that do most of the work in in-line skating are the gluteals (the buttocks) and the stomach muscles. Like all muscles, these two groups work best when they are warmed up. Use the stretching guide that is outlined here to get your blood pumping properly before you go out. It is also a useful regime to follow for "warming down" after you have been skating so that you are not stiff and sore the next day.

If you have suffered a sports injury in the past, seek the advice of your doctor or an osteopath before attempting in-line skating. They will advise you about the suitability of training exercises and may even suggest a special program for you to try.

When you are warming up, hold each of the following stretches for 8–10 seconds. When you are warming down, hold each stretch for 16–20 seconds. Never bounce. Repeat each exercise four or five times, each time gently pushing yourself to your limit, and gradually beyond. Do not over-stretch, and be aware of your limits, especially when your body is cold.

Lower Body

Begin from the lower body and work upward, starting with the muscles at the back of the lower leg.

→ **Calf** – Standing with one leg in front of the other, support your weight by pressing your hands against a wall. Gradually straighten the rear leg, bringing your heel down until you feel the tension in the calf muscle. Hold and repeat the exercise.

→ **Inner calf** – Repeat the above exercise but with a slightly flexed knee and ankle. This will help to stretch the inner calf muscles.

→ **Hamstring** – This is a modified version of a hurdler's stretch. Sit on a comfortable surface with one leg straight out. Bring your other foot up toward your groin. Reach toward the furthest foot with both hands until you feel the stretch. Repeat with the other leg.

→ **Quads** – Support yourself by holding the back of a chair or against a wall with one hand. Lift the opposite leg so that your knee is raised toward your chest, take your ankle in the other hand. Slowly lower your knee toward the ground, making sure that you do not arch backward or forward. Repeat with the other leg.

→ **Adductor** – Stand with your feet wider apart than the width of your shoulders and gradually reach down, bending at one knee, to grasp one ankle. Feel the stretch on the inside of the straightened leg. Repeat this on the other side.

→ **Gluteal** – The yoga stretch – Sit down and adopt a "yoga" position, crossing over one leg and positioning the foot by the opposite knee. From this position, fully twist the top half of your body, bringing your opposite shoulder around toward the bent knee. Lock in your arm with the raised knee and pull in the knee to produce the stretch. Repeat on the other side.

Upper Body

Although your lower body will be doing all the hard work, your lower back and waist must be adequately prepared to cope with the torque.

→ **Rotations** – The best stretching exercise for the three muscles in the stomach – the internal, external, and transverse obliques – is rotation. Simply rotating at the waist will provide an adequate stretch, but it must be done carefully to avoid strain. Gently rotate first to the left, then to the right, to the limit of your movement, keeping the pelvis facing forward.

→ **Side bends** – As well as warming the transverse obliques, side bends will open up the lower ribs to improve lung capacity. Stand with your feet shoulder-width apart and reach down to each side in turn, remembering not to lean forward or backward.

First Techniques

Whether you consider yourself a cautious or an aggressive learner, a great way of gaining confidence on your skates and to get a feel for the way they perform before you move to asphalt, is to begin on a deep surface, such as grass or, if you prefer, a carpet in the comfort of your home or office. Warming up your skills on grass is a great way to begin each time anyway, at least until you are confident enough to clip on and skate straight away on the pavement.

Basic Training

Grass-edged sidewalks and cycleways made from smooth asphalt are ideal places to begin, allowing you to move easily from one surface to another. You can use the grass as a safe escape, which will boost your confidence and help you to progress faster. It is worth giving some thought to local areas where you could begin skating. Ideally, the grass should be short, but quite lush – that is, not patchy or too dry, so that the wheels won't gather any speed. Make sure that it is a safe place, and that you have access rights. If you cannot find any grass, or a similar surface that will slow you, get as much practice on carpet before you go directly onto asphalt.

Starting and stopping on skates are the most basic skills, and going through the motions on grass will give you the best idea of how the skates are likely to behave later. The amount of time you spend on grass will depend on how soon you feel comfortable enough to move on. Don't expect to perfect your techniques on grass. Remember that you are not aiming to become really expert on grass, it is simply a means of getting to the asphalt, which is where the action is!

Putting skates on is also easier on grass. With one skate on, the grass will help you balance while you put on the other. If you wish, you can try getting a feel for the way the skates will behave by putting only one on, then rolling it around for a while.

The Ready Position

Once you are standing with both skates on, wearing all the necessary protective gear, the first thing to learn and understand is the Ready Position (see above). There will be frequent references to this and other basic skills throughout this book, but the Ready Position is the most important.

The Ready Position is your starting position, the safe "neutral gear" from which nearly all moves on in-line skates should come. It prepares you for a balanced, well-postured approach to the subsequent skills that you will learn. Balance and posture are the keys to in-line skating.

Look at the demonstrations. Make sure that your feet are about shoulder-width apart and that your toes are pointing forward. Your ankles, knees, and hips should be slightly flexed,

The Ready Position seen from the side. Your knees and ankles should be slightly flexed, your hands forward, and your weight over the balls of your feet.

as should your waist, to keep your weight over the balls of your feet. Remember that you are trying to discover your best and most balanced stance. Put your hands out in front of you, and keep your head up. Try to relax, ready for your new experiences.

It would be surprising if you did not feel nervous at this point. When we do anything for the first time, our bodies do not know how to perform. They can only go on what they have done before, so it is natural to fidget and experiment until the best possible point of balance is achieved. Try leaning forward, attempting to touch your toes, and see what the limit is before you fall forward; do the same backward. Flex your knees and ankles forward, bending and straightening at least 10 times until you feel more comfortable in your new world.

Scissoring

Stay in the Ready Position and begin to feel for the roll of the skates. On grass, you will have to roll them against the extra resistance backward and forward, using your feet. Do this for a few minutes at a time, as lightly or as aggressively as you want. These simple exercises will teach you much more than you think. Notice how your knees and ankles flex as you shuffle the skates. Try to do it in smooth, rhythmic motions, and you can even count as you do: "One, two, one, two."

Try lifting one skate, then the other. Remember to keep the leg on which you are balanced well flexed, then try waggling your foot in the air, put it down again, and so on. Get to know what you have strapped to your feet, and "make friends" with your new partners – it won't be long before they feel like extensions of your body.

Once comfortable with the Ready Position, you can have a go at scissoring.

Inner edges

Center edges

Outer edges

Edges

If you follow the techniques correctly, you will automatically use the appropriate edges of the wheels to execute a maneuver, changing from one to another constantly, without much conscious thought. However, it is important that you know the difference, so that if you have any problems, you can determine where you might be going wrong. References to the edges of your wheels could mean one of three positions: center edges, inner edges, or outer edges.

Look at the photographs and note the three positions. Most of the time you will use the center edges and inner edges. You will need to use the inner edges for all early skating techniques; the outer edges are really used only in later turning and more skillful techniques.

Experiment between the three: while standing still, look down at your skates and move onto the center edges – your knees and feet should be level, leaning neither in nor out. To get onto the inner edges, stand with your feet further apart and roll your knees in toward each other. The outer edges are a little more difficult to get onto and will feel the most unnatural. Roll your knees away from each other. The outer edges will be used on only one skate at a time when turning. Try rolling your knees from side to side, simulating a parallel skiing turn, to see what is involved.

Lead and Shadow Skate

Most people have a stronger and/or more dominant leg. It is important to identify whether it is your right or left leg, not only so that you can understand the explanations used in this book, but also so that you can determine which skate should have the heel brake.

The dominant side is referred to in this book as the lead, and you will come across references to the lead leg, lead foot, or lead skate. The leg that follows is referred as the shadow. To identify accurately which is which, stand with your feet together and ask someone to push you gently from behind. The leg that steps out to stop you falling is your lead leg. (This is the same procedure that is used to discover whether you are "regular" or "goofy" when you go surfing or snowboarding.)

V-walk

Now you have tried a few static exercises, it is time to walk with the skates a little. This is known as the V-walk, and it is the fundamental process in learning the skating action.

Begin with your feet in a simple V-position. Look down at your skates and position them with the heels (the rear of the skates) almost touching. Keep your feet in the V-position, then pick up one foot and put it down ahead of you. Repeat with the other foot. Now you are V-walking. Concentrate on keeping the skates in the V-position – you should feel a bit like a duck walking! Practice the V-walk forward, staying flexed and with your weight forward and hands in front of you. While on grass you will not be rolling much, if at all, but when you are on asphalt, this action will get you moving. Be aware that when you start to roll, your body's natural reaction will be to lean backward, which is wrong. Practice remaining flexed and forward.

Well-executed V-walking should easily propel you forward on the asphalt, but the aim is not to be a perfect V-walker. The purpose is to get you moving and set you on the easy route to performing stroking (see pages 46–47).

Stroking is elementary skating, and you can get a feel for it on grass. Progress from the V-walk by pushing sideways on the inner edges of the wheels as you move from one skate to the other. This sideways movement will propel you forward faster, but you don't have to push too hard. Balance and stroke gently. On grass you will not achieve much, if any, propulsion, but it is good practice.

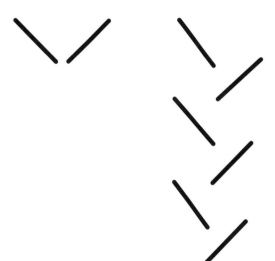

From the V-position lift one foot in the air.

Keeping to the V-position, place the foot down in front of you.

Make sure your first foot is firmly on the ground before lifting the second.

Repeat the process, moving forward each time.

Falling and Getting Up

The reality of in-line skating is that the surface is hard when you fall. Ice skaters can slide when they fall on ice, but in-line skaters cannot, which is why you must always wear protective gear (see pages 24–25). For your own safety and enjoyment, stick to the advice given.

Don't let the fear of falling and hurting yourself deter you from sharing in the fun of in-line skating, however. Millions of people across the world enjoy the sport, and falling is a natural part of the learning process. Accept that there is a risk, and learn from your falls.

Falling down can give you quite a shock, but with the right protective gear you will prevent hurting yourself as well.

You may fall for a variety of reasons, some obvious, some not. The commonest reason for falling is, in fact, fear: your mind loses control over what your body is doing, and it is often at this point that your body reacts by falling over. However, if you find yourself with time to think about falling, you also have time to think about recovering. Learn to stay calm and attempt to recover rather than panic and fall.

If you do fall, don't feel ashamed or embarrassed, and never think that you have failed. Everyone who has ever been on in-line skates has probably fallen at some time or other, and often it can be more of a positive than a negative experience. Knowing what it feels like to fall can be reassuring – the knowledge lets you get on with having fun.

There is a recommended technique for falling, and for the order in which various parts of your body come into contact with the ground, but in reality, falling tends to happen so quickly that you will not have time to apply a technique. Nevertheless, it is worth practicing going through the motions so that when you do fall you react automatically. Get used to wearing your pads and learn how they can help you. **Remember the order – knees, elbows, wrists.**
One of the most usual ways of falling is backward. It is wrong to lean back when skating, but many of us do. The body's instinct is to lean backward – we do it naturally if we want to slow down when we are running or walking, especially downhill. Digging our heels in does not work in skating. If you try it, you will fall backward, normally onto your hips or buttocks. Padded shorts are available to protect these vulnerable areas, so if you think you will need the extra protection, get some.

When you have fallen, there is a simple sequence to follow for getting upright again.

1 *Sequence for getting up. Swing your knees around so that you can get into a kneeling position.*

1 Sequence for falling. Relaxing as you go, drop onto your knee pads.

2 Keep your fingers up, as your elbow and wrist guards slide along the ground.

2 Raise one leg and place the wheels of the skate on the ground.

3 Place both hands on the knee of this leg and, using your arms to help, straighten both legs, bringing your other skate around.

4 For stability, move into the a V-position (see page 41), or T-position (see page 44) before moving off again.

Stand still in a T-position to prevent the wheels from rolling unnecessarily.

First Strides

When you leave the grass and move onto asphalt, the ideal surface should be smooth and flat, and free from traffic and pedestrians. The smoother it is, the better.

Stop! Before you go any further, it is important to remember that you have not learned how to stop. Learning to stop immediately is not necessary if you are learning in an area that allows you to come to a natural stop, if you are skating on grass, or if you are accompanied by an instructor or a friend who can catch you at the slow speeds at which you will be traveling during these early stages. You should not be traveling forward at more than walking speed during these first strides. However, if you need to learn how to stop before you gather any speed, turn to page 48 and study the instructions in First Stop pages 48–50.

T-Position

When you are on a flat surface you shouldn't roll away, but wheels are not designed to remain still, especially if your feet are fidgeting. So it is worth learning the T-position, a simple method of staying still when the wheels want to roll.

Quite simply, place your skates in a position representing the letter T as shown in the photograph [above]. They should be at right angles, with the heel of one skate halfway along the inside of the other.

On an uneven surface or a slight incline, the exact position of the skates will be critical to prevent you from rolling away. The back skate should be at exactly 90 degrees to the slope and should be the skate furthest downhill. As you progress, this technique will become second nature, and you will find that you can stand still just almost anywhere on any slope.

The ideal learning surface is smooth and flat, and free of traffic and pedestrians.

1 *V-walk sequence on tarmac. Keeping you r weight forward, repeat the sequence shown on page 43.*

Spot Check

Just as you learned to understand the likely behavior of the skates on grass, repeat a few of the exercises to understand their action on asphalt. First, adopt the Ready Position: flexed at knees, ankles, and waist, and with your arms forward in a well-balanced stance.

Gently shuffle your skates back and forth, allowing your knees and ankles to flex normally with each movement. Repeat this until you feel comfortable with the way the wheels move. Having wheels under your feet for the first time on asphalt is a unique experience, so take some time to get used to the sensation.

Become accustomed to the edges on asphalt, too. The differences between inner, center, and outer edges are even more noticeable than on grass.

V-walk

From a Ready Position, repeat the motions learned on grass. Adopt the V-position, then step forward, roughly on the center edges. Remember to keep your weight forward, remaining flexed and as relaxed as possible at all times.

Using slow, rhythmical steps, V-walk forward, keeping your toes pointing outward and heels together. Remember, you should feel like a duck walking!

If your V-walk has been satisfactorily executed, you should find yourself rolling gently, enjoying the pleasure of your first small strides on in-line skates. You might feel that control has passed into the hands of gravity, but don't worry! You will develop methods of control as you progress. For now, enjoy the motion and freedom of skating, albeit at a slow speed.

As we have seen, V-walking is only a means of learning to skate, so don't perfect it, but do practice it. Repeat the exercise if you have trouble in propelling yourself forward. (See Troubles on pages 54–57 for difficulties.)

2 *Remember to keep relaxed but flexed at all times.*

3 *Keep your movements slow and rhythmical until you get a good grasp of it.*

4 *Repeat the steps several times, keeping your toes pointing outward and heels together.*

Stroking

V-walking easily becomes stroking. If you have practiced this on grass, you will not have experienced the sensation of rolling, but you will, ideally, have an understanding of what is required to perform this relatively easy technique. Stroking is really a slower form of striding, the technique that you are working toward.

Until you understand what you are doing, the most effective way to learn is to follow set patterns. At first, these might seem very mechanical, but as you practice, you will repeat the patterns often enough that they will become automatic. To make it easy, the techniques have been described as three-step routines, which break down the maneuvers into digestible chunks, and to simplify other techniques, three-step routines will be used throughout

the book. Once you have adopted the maneuvers naturally and they become automatic and flowing, you will be able to discard the sequence routine.

From the Ready Position, begin to V-walk, with your weight forward. When you have gained a little momentum, place your skates parallel to each other and then begin a routine of propelling yourself forward by scooting one skate at a time. The difference this time is that, by tilting the skate and pushing it gently out to the side, you will produce more energy and, therefore, more significant forward motion. Make one stroke at a time with each leg, bringing the skates back parallel to each other and into a moving Ready Position. This will give you time to check your balance between each scoot, preparing you for the next stroke.

1   *From the Ready Position, begin to V-walk to gain some momentum, keeping your weight forward.*

2   *Stay on the inner edges of the wheels and scoot the skate out sideways. Make sure the skate goes to the side and not backward, behind you.*

Between each stroke you should experience your first taste of gliding. Enjoy this sensation, even though it is slow: it is one of the sensations that in-line skaters live for! The sequence for the V-walk is:

1 **Ready**

2 **Stroke**

3 **Regroup**

Practice stroking and develop a feel for balance on the move. Again, stroking is really only a building block. It will help develop your confidence and take you toward real skating, where stroking and gliding combine to become striding. Once you've had a taste of a little speed, you might be tempted to move on swiftly and get a little more wind in your hair… but, it is a good idea to learn how to stop.

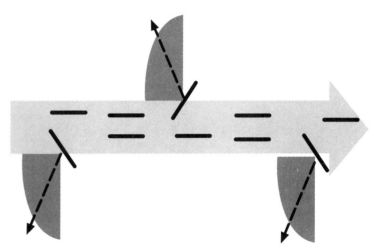

3 *Regroup by bringing the skate back in so that your skates are parallel with each other.*

4 *Your skates must be parallel when you Glide so that you can control your movements at this faster speed.*

5 *Repeat the move with the other leg, then the first, until you have built up a smooth rhythm.*

First Stop

In-line skating really becomes fun when you know how to stop. The excitement of motion is easy to understand, but the fear inside prevents us from enjoying it until we know we have it under control. Knowing how to control your speed now will help you learn faster as your confidence increases.

There are several ways of slowing down and stopping, but it is worth pointing out that there is no such thing as a sudden stop. Anything that moves has momentum, which resists any attempt to bring the object to a halt. Consequently, it takes time and distance to stop. You will be learning a new stopping method in a new world, so give yourself plenty of time to get it right.

Like all the moves you have learned so far, don't try to perfect the technique of stopping, but perfect the stop. If you find that you are not slowing or do not stop where you intend, you need more practice. Satisfy yourself that you can achieve a good stop to match the speeds you aspire to and the places you will go. Practice stopping regularly, even though at times you may think you can get way with it. Stop first, then you can go!

Rollerblade's® ABT™ brake shown above and other specific braking systems have made braking easier.

Heel Stop

There are several ways of slowing down and stopping, some more flamboyant than others, but the first and most important method of stopping is the heel stop, which has proved to be the most effective and quickest way of controlling speed for the majority of beginners. It is a reliable technique that requires the minimum of balancing skills.

The objective is to create sufficient resistance between the rubber brake and the ground to slow you down and bring you to a halt. This important maneuver requires commitment. To understand what your brake should be doing, take a close look at it. Remove the skate from your foot and feel it with your fingers. Also, make sure that the brake is on the lead skate (see page 40).

The heel stop maneuver requires you to use another new component – scissoring. Only from the scissor will you be able to locate the brake. Remember: no scissor, no brake. Get this right and the rest is easy. Scissoring the skates is not only an essential part of the heel stop, it is also a fundamental element in all aspects of skating, including forms of turning, other stopping methods, and riding on uneven surfaces.

Scissoring the skates simply means sliding one skate parallel to, but in front of, the other, keeping your weight over the balls of both feet. This action will improve your balance, which will be further enhanced as your body naturally lowers

1 *From a gliding Ready Position begin to scissor your lead skate.*

Practice the three-stage sequence on grass first if you wish.

its center of gravity. Holding a good Ready Position is the key to maintaining a relaxed stance and will help you to align your weight correctly.

Practice with both feet. This is very similar to what you were doing when you first began to skate on asphalt. You should find it easier and more natural to slide your lead foot forward, which is exactly what you need to do to reach the brake.

The final stage of the sequence is the most difficult, but it is easy when the scissor is performed properly. From the scissor, take the weight off your lead skate (now in front) so that you are able to lift up your toe. Lift your toe until the rubber brake pad makes contact with the ground. Lean on the back cuff of the lead skate by straightening your leg and sinking down onto it. This action will be easier if your shadow leg is well flexed. Imagine you are "cracking a nut" under the brake pad. If the rubber squeals as it brakes, this is a good sign; the louder the squeal, the faster you'll stop!

Brand Rollerblade® skates use ABT* (Active Brake Technology). Other makes use other braking systems. With the ABT system, there is no need to lift the toe – the toe-up stage – in order to locate the brake. The simple action of Scissoring should automatically bring you to a stop because there is a lever between the rear cuff and the brake pad.

Static Practice

Practice the heel stop sequence on the spot, aiming to make each movement smooth, until you feel you will be able to perform it on the move. The sequence is:

1 **Ready**
2 **Scissor**
3 **Toe-up**

Say the sequence to yourself as you perform each action.

2   *Transfer more weight to your back leg as you scissor.*

3   *Check your balance and begin to lift the toe until the rubber brake pad comes into contact with the ground.*

4   *Lean on the back cuff of the lead skate by straightening your leg and sinking down onto it.*

Heel Stop – On the Move

Begin slowly, then as you gather confidence in the effectiveness of your heel stop, you can increase the pace. The faster you can stop, the faster you can go.

Start by stroking forward to gather some momentum. Let the skates run parallel and check your Ready Position (1); scissor (2), holding and checking your position; stay down, then toe-up (3). Commit to each stage of the maneuver.

Applying more pressure to the rubber brake involves the following: a low body position, a great scissor, and, once you have lifted your toe, increased force on the rear cuff of the skate. This will produce increased resistance between pad and ground. Straightening your lead leg in the toe-up position is necessary to apply increased cuff pressure – but don't stand up! Use the muscles in your legs to create that resistance and stay down!

Remember that the gradual application of pressure will bring you to a stop. As you progress and gain experience, you will learn to predict when you will need to stop and, therefore, when to begin braking. Very quickly, you will be doing it without thinking about it.

Skating the Grass

If you are learning on asphalt bordered by grass, where it is possible to roll directly onto the grass without having to mount a curb, skating the grass is a great stopping technique. It is probably easier than the heel stop.

Once you are rolling, move into a scissors position, but keep your weight slightly back so that you won't fall forward when the wheels are slowed by the greater resistance of the grass. Then allow the wheels to come to a natural stop.

Never skate the grass if it is wet, especially if it is muddy. The wheels will simply dig in and you will go flying. In contrast, be aware that very dry grass may perform like asphalt, providing little or no resistance. Faced with either of these circumstances, work to perfect the heel stop.

If you find yourself in a situation where the grass is damp or wet and you have no time to use another stopping technique, or if you need to cross a small area of grass between sections of asphalt, simply run onto it. In other words, if your skates stop suddenly, you can avoid a fall by running out the momentum and stopping as you would if you were wearing normal shoes.

1 *From a Ready Position begin gently stroking.*

2 *After a few strokes, begin to drive off the stroking skate and advancing the body and the leg onto the other gliding skate.*

3 *At the end of that stroke, instantly transfer the weight onto the other skate and repeat the action.*

Now rotate . . . make sure you edge properly with the inside and out-side edges as shown here.

Striding

Having grasped the basics of controlling your speed, the desire to go faster will come as no surprise. Striding is a more dynamic version of stroking, where the combination of a stroke and a glide becomes a stride. Striding is the action from which all new methods will develop. Once you have mastered striding, you are really skating.

The difference between stroking and striding is that you will be moving faster; there is no longer a delay between each stroke, and no time for checking balance in a moving Ready Position. Striding is the continuous action of stroking with one leg, while balancing and Gliding on the other. The three-step sequence is:

1 **Stroke right and glide**
2 **Stroke left and glide**
3 **Repeat**

From a Ready Position, begin gently stroking. After a few strokes, lean forward more, driving off the stroking skate and advancing your body and leg onto a new gliding skate. Maintain a striding rhythm: scooting out one skate, gliding onto the other; scooting out one skate, gliding onto the

other, and so on. Make sure that you use your inner edges of the wheels as the platform, keeping them in a V-configuration. If the scooting skate faces forward, the wheels will spin and you will not advance. A common mistake at this stage of learning to skate is to push backward, when you should be pushing sideways. If necessary go back to a V-walk and practice stroking.

Striding at slower speeds will help you understand skating. In the following chapter, you will discover how to increase your striding speed as your body learns to adopt a Dynamic Ready Position for more freedom of movement.

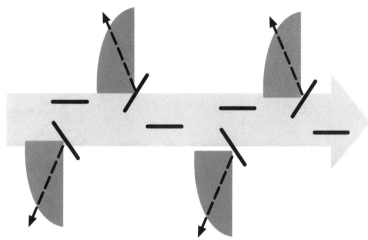

4 *Maintain a striding rhythm, stroking and sweeping on one skate, gliding on the other.*

5 *Stroking and sweeping out the other skate, glide onto the other.*

First Turn

Learning to steer your skates is probably more important in developing freedom on in-line skates than stopping. This is because steering away from trouble in a hurry is easier than trying to stop in a hurry. (However, this does not mean that stopping is a skill that can be skipped!)

There are several techniques for turning. The most basic is the A-frame Turn, so called because of the A-shape position adopted by the body to perform it. This maneuver is really only a building block in your understanding of how the edges of the wheels work, and how to make them turn. Once you understand their performance, you will be able to experiment and execute a less systematic way of edging and turning, as you will learn in future techniques.

The A-frame Turn cannot really be appreciated when you are stationary, because you need momentum to take the skates in a new direction. However, you can practice the A-frame stance and edging skills, which are necessary for taking you into the corner.

Adopting an A-frame stance is simply a matter of moving your legs apart until you reach the inner edges of the skates. At this point, if you apply pressure to one edged skate, it will turn. What may be confusing is that the left skate will take you right, and vice versa. Edging the skates is a preparation for changing direction; adding pressure to one of those edges will produce the turn.

Before you attempt your first turn, decide which way you want to go. It is often best to start by using your lead skate, but this is not essential, because learning to turn in both directions is important.

The sequence for the A-frame Turn is:

1 **Ready**
2 **A-frame**
3 **Pressure**

Having gained momentum, from the Ready Position (1) allow the skates to drift apart until you find the edges and are in the A-frame position (2). Apply pressure (3) to one foot,

1 *From the Ready Position allow your skates to drift apart.*

2 *When you have found the edges, you will have adopted an A-frame stance.*

3 *Apply pressure to one foot and point it slightly in the direction in which you want to travel.*

pointing it slightly in the new direction of travel. Think of applying pressure by pressing your toes down on an imaginary button. Continue turning until you are heading in the direction you require, then release the pressure and straighten out.

Try this several times, and in both directions, until you get the hang of it. You may find that you have turned in a different manner, perhaps more like a parallel turn or a lunge turn as described on pages 64–67. Again, don't try to perfect the technique of turning; instead, perfect the turn. Try to understand the type of turn you have executed because they all have specific advantages and disadvantages in more advanced skating and you need to be aware of these.

The A-frame Turn is the last maneuver to learn in this first group of techniques. Refer to Troubles if you are having any outstanding difficulties. If not, move onto the next chapter, Moving and Improving. That is where new speeds and new destinations will make your eyes water!

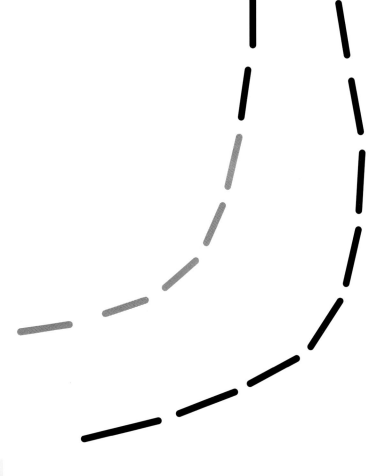

4 *Steer around and finish the turn.*

Troubles

Balance Difficulties

Symptom

Unable to stand or keep still

Body shaking

Problem

Poor posture

High anxiety, too tense

Reason

New balance experience for body; it is quite normal to experience balance difficulties when you are learning to skate; almost all new skaters have this problem. In-line skating requires a basic level of balance, but only enough to enable you to walk. From that point, you will develop new levels of balance for skating as your body's natural instincts react automatically, adapting to the changes in your situation. So don't be put off; give yourself plenty of time.

Use a wall, tree, or, best of all, a pole to hold on to while you practice balancing exercises.

Difficulty Gathering Momentum or Speed

Symptom

Hardly moving forward, despite action from legs and feet

Problem

Poor stroking technique: feet and skates too straight; toes not turned out and heels not turned in enough to form a V-shape.

Reason

Not enough use of inner edges for grip

Trying to push feet directly backward, forcing skates to straighten and losing the V-shape

Weight not central over skates, creating imbalance

Excessive upper body movement

Stroking action too fast and without rhythm

Most learning problems stem from a poor ready position. Standing too straight, as shown here, makes it more likely that you will fall backward.

Correction

Correct Ready Position. Make sure that you are properly flexed at all leg joints (ankles, knees, and hips) and at your waist. Press your shins firmly against the front cuffs of your inner boots, which is a good guide to how flexed your ankles should be. Drop your shoulders and keep your hands still; try to focus on relaxing the muscles in your whole body.

Bend lower

Check that your weight is evenly balanced over both feet when setting off in the Ready Position.

See your hands in front of you. This will help balance your stance. Don't look directly at them; you will need to be looking ahead for safety.

Don't lean too far forward or too far back. Adopt a flexed stance over the balls of your feet; get comfortable on your skates.

Practice your balancing skills without skates on to strengthen and prepare your muscles before you go skating. Bending and flexing, as well as standing on one leg at a time, will help enormously.

Mind Over Matter

Don't be too fearful or distressed about the consequences of falling over and possibly embarrassing yourself. Approach the learning experience in a positive way, focusing on how to help your body balance better. Negative thinking will create larger problems, taking energy away from the business of learning and having fun.

Try to think of your feet: where they are, what they are feeling, and how they are working to keep you balanced. Consider that your brain is trying to communicate directly with your feet to achieve an understanding for balance, and that it requires a calm, relaxed body between to achieve an effective link.

A mistake often made by beginners is "walking" the skate behind, as shown here. Instead, you should Stroke sideways to create forward momentum.

Correction

Practice V-walk, concentrating on keeping your toes out and heels in.

Maintain a more flexed position, bending lower, but keeping weight over the balls of your feet. Work on your Ready Position (see Balance Difficulties, opposite). Go back to grass if necessary.

Slow down the stroking action; work on a steady rhythm. Count "One, two; one, two" as you stroke with each leg to help establish a rhythm.

Calm your body movement, focusing more on the action of your feet.

Stopping Difficulties

Symptom	Problem	Reason
Not slowing or stopping	Poor use or understanding of heel stop technique	Poor balance in Ready Position
No control over speed	No control or pressure on brake pad	No scissor technique or too narrow a gap between skates
		Weight balanced too much on front skate in scissor
		Back leg not flexed enough
		Brake located on wrong skate
		Lack of commitment to maneuver
		Not enough pressure on back cuff of front skate when you toe-up
		Pressure applied too quickly

If you find you are not achieving your moves, seek help from an instructor.

Turning Troubles

Symptom	Problem	Reason
Unable to make a turn in either direction	A-frame not distinct enough; skates too close together	Failure to find inner edges of wheels
Unable to turn in one direction	Leaning instead of edging in A-frame	Lack of pressure applied to edge

Do not rely just on your body for turning. It will also depend on the action of your feet.

Correction

Continue to work on balance skills as described.

Perfect the scissor technique, making the scissor as wide as you comfortably can (go back to grass if necessary); slide your front skate forward and back skate backward, and keep your weight centralized and over the balls of your feet while scissoring.

Practice the three-step sequence while you are stationary.

Stick your backside out as you toe-up on the front skate, and tip your chest downward to help straighten your leg; feel the calf muscles working in your leg as you toe-up effectively; work the legs more at the toe-up stage; do not tense your body and force the maneuver

Keep your hands pointing forward and balanced throughout.

Practice the three-step sequence repeatedly until the brake is creating resistance with the ground.

Apply pressure to the brake pad over a longer period, increasing the angle of toe-up throughout maneuver.

Make sure that the brake pad is located on the shadow skate.

Set yourself stopping targets, skating faster and stopping sooner to improve your stopping ability.

Correction

Spread your feet further apart to find the inner edges of wheels

Keep your body centrally balanced and focus on the turning action of your feet

Flex your knee and press down your toe to apply pressure

04   Moving and Improving

Moving and Improving

The basic learning techniques described in First Strides will have taught you how to start, stop, and turn. Most importantly, your balance should have developed so that you are able to repeat each maneuver with a good degree of consistency and confidence. The new techniques you will discover in this chapter will add to those basic skills and provide a positive learning experience. They will take you to an intermediate stage in the development of your skating, showing you how to move faster and less systematically, as more fluid movements are needed to perform these more dynamic skills.

Understanding of the word "dynamic" is the key in this chapter, for much of the learning will be done in motion. These new techniques cannot be understood unless you have sufficient momentum to experience them, or even make them happen.

You must allow yourself plenty of room for error when learning these intermediate skills, for it is only when you push yourself to the extremes of your present abilities that you will fully understand how they should be done and, more importantly, what they should feel like.

Dynamic Ready Position

So that you can move more freely, you must begin to appreciate the core needs for good balance, no longer relying on the "staged" Ready Position, which inhibits real freedom of movement. The basic Ready Position provided you with the foundations for developing good balance, but the Dynamic Ready Position occurs on the move, and it is the position from which all your moves will be executed. By now, you should be beginning to develop a natural appreciation of the need for flexed ankles and knees, for your body to be flexed at the waist, and for keeping your weight over the balls of the feet. The Dynamic Ready Position is not a specific learned technique, but a natural stance that will become more prominent as you improve. You should be aware of being lower and more responsive to the changing environment.

Your hands and arms should move from the static position of straight out in front of you, to a more active and more dynamic role, providing the balance and counterbalance that will allow you to perform faster moves successfully.

Skating Venues

From a restricted learning area, you can be more adventurous and move to an improved skating environment. From now on, you may encounter many new surroundings and obstacles. Once you have learned faster striding, and more effective stopping and turning, you may choose a route that involves skating on cycleways, stepping on and off curbs, maneuvering around pedestrians and cycles, as well as changes in skating surface.

Equipment

At this point, it is worth evaluating the quality of your skates or, more importantly, their wheels and bearings. If the wheels and bearings are poor, you will not be able to gain the speeds required to move and improve. Refer to the discussion of basic equipment on pages 20–35.

1 *From a basic stride, begin to extend your body, stretching further onto the gliding skate. Your legs will perform a much more explosive action, with the power leg almost straight at the end of each stride, so that you maximize the power in the movement and create more speed.*

Allow your arms to swing with each stride in dynamic striding.

Dynamic Striding

An extension of basic striding, dynamic striding requires extra power and increased edging, giving you the ability to drive a longer, faster stride and so reach higher speeds. It is a constant, flowing movement that needs more assistance from your arms to create extra propulsion.

From a basic stride, begin to extend your body, stretching further onto the gliding skate. Considerably more explosive action is needed from your legs in each stride; the power leg should be almost straight at the end of each stride to maximize the power and create more speed. A well-edged skate driving sideways (not backward) is essential. Swinging both arms from side to side across your body will help with each stride (left arm straight when left leg is straight, and vice versa). The increased drive from each skate will result in an upward motion as you stride forward, and a downward motion as you transfer the weight onto the new striding leg. You will also feel as if you are following the gliding skate sideways for a brief moment, as its turned-out position takes it in its natural gliding direction. However, keep your upper body facing forward, and the opposite, new stride will follow automatically, balancing any veering that a single stride produces and enabling you to maintain steady control.

Perfecting the technique of your stride is something you can work on. This will allow you to develop a more satisfactory and more effective way of getting about, and permit you to gain more speed and, therefore, derive more enjoyment from the glide. You can congratulate yourself when you reach this stage, for this is solid skating. Furthermore, you will soon appreciate the fitness benefits that in-line skating can bring, as you stride happily from one place to another, and back again, in a lung expanding, heart-pounding workout, which will also give you the experience necessary for hockey, racing, and all other applications of in-line skating.

To progress further in your striding, refer to power striding on pages 82–83. This is a great technique that will squeeze every ounce of energy out of each stride!

2 *The extra movement should allow you to relax your arms and swing them from side to side across your body.*

3 *Keep your left arm straight, when your left leg is straight and vice versa.*

4 *Make sure that each skate drives sideways and not backward.*

Swizzles

To swizzle, or make a "lemon" as it often called, will propel you from a stationary position and requires power from your thighs. Swizzles are great skill-building exercises and, although they have no direct use in everyday skating, they will help you get a better feeling for the edge and pressure changes under your feet.

Swizzle properly and the skates drive out sideways, creating forward momentum that will take them through a "half-lemon" arc. Then, in one continuous move, you pull them back together again to complete the swizzle and finish off the lemon shape. Link all of these movements together, concentrating throughout on the sensations you feel in your feet. As well as being a technique for learning backward skating, practicing swizzles give you coordination and control for many future techniques.

The sequence for performing a Swizzle is:

1   **V-position**
2   **Dual stroke**
3   **Regroup**

Begin in a well-flexed V-position (1), with your knees leaning in more so that you are on your inner edges. With your weight on both feet, dual stroke (2) both skates simultaneously, driving downward by using the muscles in your thighs. As you propel forward, regroup (3) by pulling the skates back in. Then repeat the move. Make the course your skates take follow the outline of a lemon fruit. Swizzle forward until you are able to link four or five swizzles together.

4   *As you propel yourself forward, regroup your skates.*

5   *Bring your skates back to the V-position.*

6   *Then, start again, keeping your movements flowing.*

1 Start in a well-flexed V-position, with your knees leaning in slightly so that you are on the inner edges of your wheels.

2 With your weight on both feet, dual stroke both skates at the same time, driving downward by using your thigh muscles.

3 Your skates will follow the shape of a lemon. Spread them wide as shown here.

7 Remember to drive downward with your thigh muscles.

8 Practice your forward swizzle several times over.

9 You should be able to link four or five swizzles together.

Turning the Glide

Parallel Turning

The A-frame turn learned in the previous chapter will have given you confidence in the stability of the basic Ready Position and a feeling for turning the inner edges. However, it is a rather elementary and mechanical method of turning that is not ideal for more advanced skating.

Parallel turning gives you the flexibility to turn sharply and quickly, arming you with the ability to move more effectively, thus avoiding obstacles that you may encounter on your new travels. Parallel turning will enable you to turn both the inner and outer edges. It is also the technical foundation for slalom turning and controlling speed downhill, but the technique on hills is more akin to snow skiing than skating. Forces generated on slopes affect skates quite differently, and to control them properly can require additional techniques. Hill skating and skiing techniques are covered on pages 96–98 and 102–103.

Parallel turning is a relatively easy skill to perform. Your knees and feet both work together, edging and turning at the same time so that your skates follow parallel tracks. You will need little additional help (to begin with) from your upper body as it rotates.

The sequence for making a parallel turn is:

1	**Edge**
2	**Pressure**
3	**Rotate**

Before you attempt a Parallel turn, remind yourself of the movement needed to keep the skates parallel by rolling your knees from side to side. Also be aware of how to rotate your body by turning your shoulders and twisting from the waist into the direction of the turn.

Having chosen the direction of your turn, skate to gliding speed. Adopt a Ready Position, then edge (1) both skates so that they are parallel by leaning your knees and pointing

1   *Choose the direction in which you want to turn, then skate to Gliding speed.*

2   *Adopt a Ready Position, then edge both skates until they are parallel by leaning your knees and pointing your toes in the direction of the turn.*

3   *Now rotate your shoulders to help you complete the move. Make sure that you edge properly with the outer edges of your skates.*

your toes in the direction of the turn. This action should automatically place the wheels on their outer and inner edges (2). Now rotate (3) your shoulders as practiced to assist the move. Make sure that you edge properly with your outer edged skate. Try to relax as you turn and follow the movement through. Reset the wheels edges to center by bringing your knees and shoulders back to the level to bring you straight again.

If you are having problems in initiating the turn, start in a scissor position and move into the turn prescribed by your lead skate – that is, if your left skate is the lead, go left, and vice versa.

Practice one turn at a time and build it into your skating repertoire. Steer sharply or gently, and experiment with the type of turns you can make in both directions. Parallel turning will also develop the skills needed for crossovers, the hockey stop, and the mighty power slide.

4 *Try to relax as you turn.*

5 *Finish the turn, maintaining the flow of your movements.*

Lunge Turn

When you are making a parallel turn, steer sharply, deep-setting the edges and pulling most of your weight onto your inside leg. This is a lunge turn, which is very useful for emergency steering and moving rapidly from one direction to another.

It is best to start this maneuver from a scissor. Set your edges at an extreme angle, but rather than just rotating your upper body into the turn, lean at the same extreme angle as the wheel edges. See how far you can lean without falling; you'll be amazed at the angle.

Slalom Turns

Linked parallel turns become slalom turns. When it is performed well, slalom turning is a superb sensation, allowing you to control the gravitational forces affecting all edges as you flow from one side to another. Later, you will adapt this technique to control your speed downhill, but the forces will be greater and, your technique must be precise.

The slalom turn is a combination of edge, pressure, and skate steering using your feet, in a continuous rhythm. Rotation of the upper body is not as important, but it can help you to link the turns in the early stages. However, you will find that rotating the shoulders from side to side will make you unstable and ungainly. Therefore, as you become more in tune with the performance of the edges of the skates, you should work to reduce excessive body and hip movement, which only interferes with more advanced turning techniques.

1 *Slalom turn. Assume a steady gliding ready position and initiate your first parallel turn.*

2 *Edge into the turn, apply pressure to the wheels by flexing your knees and ankles and pointing your toes into the turn.*

3 *When you have completed the arc, immediately repeat the move, in order to change direction.*

The sequence for making a slalom turn is:

1 Edge
2 Pressure
3 Repeat

From a steady gliding ready position, initiate your first parallel turn. Edge (1) into the turn, applying pressure to the wheels (2) by flexing your knees and ankles, and pointing your toes into the turn. Having completed an arc, immediately repeat the action (3), rolling your knees across and switching to the inner and outer edges on the other side. Repeat the sequence in your mind by saying: "Edge, Pressure, Repeat; Edge Pressure, Repeat," and so on.

Rather than finding your body moving from side to side, you should find it moving up and down as you roll your knees across from one side to the other. Beware of changing edges without the skates turning an arc because you have not applied pressure to the wheels.

4 *Roll your knees across so that you change to the inner and outer edges on the other side.*

5 *Continue to turn from side to side, establishing a rhythm as you move.*

Try the crossover action on the spot before you attempt to do it on the move.

Turning the Stride

The Forward Crossover

To maintain your speed as you enter a turn or even accelerate into the turn, you need to use a forward crossover. This can be used to take you in a new direction or as the most efficient way of skating in circles (around a rink, for example). When it is performed properly, the crossover is both impressive to watch and exciting to do. At speed, you will experience new turning forces and sensations as you balance on one skate while crossing the other in dynamic, consecutive movements.

Commitment is a very important factor in this relatively straightforward technique. Once you succeed at the first few, you will rapidly improve and begin to perform linked crossovers with smooth, rhythmic strides.

Before moving off, practice crossing your lead skate over the other, then follow with the rear skate crossing behind. Repeat this action. Notice that your rear skate lands forming a crude T-position, before you go into the new crossover. You may find it easier to practice on grass.

1 *From a glide, begin to lean gently in toward the inside of the turn.*

2 *Immediately cross over your skate, riding the rear skate as you lift and rotating your upper body toward the new direction of travel.*

An element of speed is required to enable you to balance properly, so you must be comfortably gliding to start the maneuver. Begin building up your confidence before you actually go into the turn with some simple exercises. Gliding straight, at a comfortable speed, lift your lead foot level with the shin of your other leg for a couple of seconds. Repeat this about 20 times, or at least until you can glide confidently with one foot off the ground, ready to go into the crossover. The sequence for making a forward crossover is:

1 **Dynamic ready position**
2 **Cross lead**
3 **Follow rear**

From a glide in the dynamic ready position (1), begin gently leaning toward the inside of the turn (whichever side is easier for your lead leg to cross over). Commit to the maneuver and, as you do, allow your upper body to rotate toward this new direction of travel. These two actions take place at the same time as you begin crossing over. Now cross lead (2) by lifting the lead skate over smoothly, placing it down, and transferring your weight onto it completely. Follow the rear (3) by bringing the rear skate from behind and back into position. Throughout the move, you will be stroking sideways with both skates to maintain speed.

Allow your arms to move freely, keeping them forward and low, and use your upper body to help determine the sharpness of the crossover turn according to the angle of its lean. The angle at which you place each skate down on its edge will also determine the angle of the turn, but don't worry too much about this at the moment.

As you improve, remember to practice the crossover in the other direction so that you can go both left and right. This will prove useful later to help you get around.

If you are finding the rossover difficult to master, refer to Moving and Improving Troubles on pages 76–79.

3 *Place the wheels of the front skate down in the direction in which you are traveling.*

4 *Transfer your weight to this skate and ride it for a few seconds, Stroking to maintain the momentum as you lift the rear skate, ready to repeat the movement.*

5 *Continue to turn, stroking and crossing as you turn the wide circle.*

Next Stops

The heel stop (see pages 48–50) is an easy, safe, and practical way of slowing and stopping. For smooth, controlled stopping in everyday skating (and reduced brake-pad wear), however, it is not always best. More advanced methods of stopping are the spin stop and the T-stop.

Spin stop

The spin stop is a great way to stop at slower speeds. When it is properly executed, it looks really cool, and it will help to save that brake pad. It is a little difficult to begin with, but with practice you will find that it is a useful action, especially at street corners!

The sequence for performing a spin stop is:

1   **Ready**
2   **Scissor**
3   **V-position**

Practice the three steps until you can perform them well on grass first. Then you can move onto the real thing.

From a gliding ready position (1), scissor (2) the skates as you would if you were preparing for a heel stop, but transfer all your weight to the lead skate. As you do, pick up the heel of the rear skate and pivot on its front wheel, rotating yourself and the skate through 180 degrees. Immediately place the skate back on the ground in a rough V-position (3). This action will automatically take you into a spin, killing momentum and bringing you to a stop. To control the sudden change of direction, as you pivot around into the

V-position, press down into your boots, deliberately flexing your knees and ankles as you do so.

T-stop

Well known as a stopping technique in ice skating, the T-stop is also widely used in in-line skating as a controlling technique at all speeds. However, it is probably more widely used for slowing down than for stopping completely.

By dragging one skate at an angle of 90 degrees behind the other on the asphalt, you will create sufficient resistance

1   *T-stop. With your weight well forward, lift your skate and take it behind you.*

1   *Spin stop. From a gliding ready position, scissor the skates as if you were about to perform a heel stop. Transfer all your weight to the lead skate.*

2   *Raise the heel of the rear skate and pivot it around on its front wheel.*

to forward motion to slow you down. To perform it well requires practice, and it is especially difficult to keep the skate at a right angle as it drags. If you put it down too early or fail to hold the wheels at 90 degrees, you may accidentally perform a spin stop. In fact, the spin stop was discovered – and is taught – because so many T-stops failed!

The sequence for making a T-stop is:

1. **Ready**
2. **Flex**
3. **Drag**

Practice this sequence on grass before moving onto asphalt.

When you are happy with the sequence of steps, begin skating and assume a gliding ready position (1). Flex (2) your left or right leg (whichever you prefer), balancing all your weight on it. With your weight well forward, lift and place the other skate behind it and at exactly 90 degrees to it. Allow the wheels to drag (3) on the ground. Hold this position until you stop or slow to the required speed.

You must perfect the T-stop before you can rely on it as a stopping technique.

2 *Place the skate at an angle of 90 degrees behind the lead skates, allowing the wheels to drag on the ground.*

3 *Hold this position until you come to a halt ...*

4 *... or until you have slowed down to the required speed.*

3 *Immediately replace the skate on the ground in a rough V-position.*

4 *You will immediately spin, with both your body and skate being rotated through 180 degrees.*

5 *The spin should have killed your speed and brought you to a complete stop.*

Backward Skating

Skating backward provides the fun and challenge of another skating dimension, but, more importantly, it helps to develop an all-round ability that will be beneficial should you take up hockey, artistic skating, or aggressive skating.

To skate backward, you must know how to swizzle properly forward (see page 62–63). This will simplify the maneuver.

Half-swizzle Backward

Initially think of skating backward as a backward half-swizzle, using just one stroking leg at a time.

The sequence for performing a backward swizzle is:

1   **Inverted V-position**
2   **Swizzle left**
3   **Swizzle right**

Point your toes in and heels out to begin in an inverted V-position (1). From well-flexed knees (it helps if you stick your backside out), swizzle left (2), driving down and sideways away from you on the toe and inner edge of the wheels to describe the "half-lemon" shape. As one skate strokes, you will automatically glide with the other. As soon as you have finished one "half-lemon," repeat the action and swizzle right (3), moving your leg backward on the other side. Adopt a rhythm and you will find your body bobbing up and down as you skate backward in a series of half-swizzles.

Over-emphasize your knee flex as you push off the new skate. As soon as you have some momentum, ease off the power and make your movements more fluid.

As you are moving backward, make sure you look over your shoulder from time to time for safety. This will also help to keep your weight centralized and over the balls of your

4   *Complete the arc of the "half lemon" shape.*

5   *Begin to repeat the half swizzle with your right leg.*

feet. Take care not to lean too far forward, since this may cause you to trip over your toes. Practice backward skating until you are confident. It will not be long, however, before you will want to turn as you travel backward. Leaning the edges will steer you, of course, but only backward crossovers will maintain the momentum as you turn.

1 *Adopt an inverted V-position – toes pointing in, and heels out.*

2 *Drive down and away from you with your left-foot.*

3 *Make sure the pressure is on the toe and inner edge of the wheels.*

6 *Drive down and away from you as before.*

7 *Complete the "half lemon" shape and repeat to get into a rhythm.*

Backward Crossover

To perform a backward crossover and so create speed requires more than a simple reversal of the forward technique. While it is very easy to begin this move, control becomes more difficult as you gather speed. If this happens, you might find yourself instinctively wanting to turn around to regain control instead of perfecting backward technique. Resist the temptation and persevere backward, working on control as you do. One of the most critical factors in the success of this maneuver is concentrating on the position in which you land the skate at each crossover, which you will ready know about from performing the forward version. The sequence for performing a backward crossover is:

1   **Lean and cross front**
2   **Land at angle and ride**
3   **Follow and cross rear**

As you are moving backward, begin to lean in towards the inside of the turn you want to make. As you do this, transfer your weight to the rear skate and lift your other foot, placing it back on the ground at the angle in which you want to travel. This is vital. Transfer your weight again, and ride this skate for a few seconds, stroking to maintain your momentum and preparing to repeat the maneuver with the other skate. Continue to turn, stroke, and crossover as you describe a wide circle, and remember to look over your shoulder as you travel.

Having successfully learned the skills in this chapter, you will have developed a natural feel for the way your skates perform, and you will know your limitations and weak points. If you have mastered the heel stop and T-stop, you should be able to cope with moderate, or even expert, routes regularly. These will test your technique to the full on varying surfaces and at varying speeds.

All the moves in the following chapter require precision in your skating, and they are a final test of your all-round recreational skating ability. More speed and power will result in more effective and more impressive skating.

1 *From a backward glide, lean into the inside of the turn.*

2 *Cross over your skate, riding the rear skate as you lift the front one.*

3 *Place the front skate on the ground so that the wheels are in the direction you want to travel.*

As you complete each crossover it is essential that you place the wheels on the ground at the angle in which you want to travel.

4 Transfer your weight and ride on this skate for a second or two, stroking to maintain your momentum. Prepare to repeat the move with the rear skate.

5 Continue to turn, stroke, and crossover as you turn a wide circle, remembering to look over your shoulder as you do.

Troubles

If you fail to turn both knees you will catch the edge, and this will stop you turning properly.

Parallel Turn

Problem	Reason	Correction
Turn not occurring	Skates stuck on center edges	Lean legs into turn
		Practice stationary edge exercises
	No steering from ankles or feet	Press toes down and rotate ankles to initiate pivot
	No help from rotation of upper body	Imagine passing a tray as you go around

Forward Crossover

Problem	Reason	Correction
Unable/unwilling to cross over leg	Lack of commitment	Lean into turn
	Not transferring weight	Flex more onto balancing leg
	Not lifting skate over properly	Practice crossover on the spot
Catching edges and almost falling	Landing skate too straight	Place landing wheels toward direction of turn and increase V-position
Turning too fast and too sharply	Progressively over-leaning in turn	More rhythmic crossovers; count, "One, two; one, two,", etc.
	Crossing over too quickly	Stand more on center edge
		Allow skate to glide forward between steps
		Lift and land skates more smoothly

Focus your energy on your feet and knees when you begin slalom turns.

Slalom Turns

Problem	Reason	Correction
Unable to link turns	Poor rhythm	Say and repeat out loud the three-step sequence: "Edge, pressure, repeat"
	Not changing edges smoothly	Roll knees more smoothly, balancing over the balls of your feet; feel more for the edge change under your feet
	Excessive upper body swing	Hold hands steady so that you can see them, and focus on steering feet in an arc

Many skaters make the mistake of relying on the rotation of the body alone to turn the skates.

Dynamic Striding

Problem	Reason	Correction
Body unstable at speed	Poor posture	Lower your body; use leg muscles more
		Flex all lower body joints
		Practice basic Ready Position
Faster Gliding difficult	Inferior bearings and/or wheels	Upgrade bearings and/or wheels
Skates wobble and feel unstable	Ill-fitting skates and/or poor-quality shell	Check skates are correct size
		Consider quality of skates and upgrade if necessary

Spin Stop

Problem	Reason	Correction
Unable to lift heel	Too much weight on rear foot	Practice scissor, balancing on front leg only
	Leaning too far back	Flex front knee
	Not moving forward onto front skate	Push hands forward more
Losing balance halfway	Standing too high	Revise Ready Position
	Poor basic balance	Practice stationary balance exercises over front foot
		Practice three-step sequence while stationary
Not spinning	Rear skate landing badly	Practice three-step sequence while stationary
	Wheels catch halfway	Place wheels down in V-position
	No final shoulder rotation	"Pass the tray" as you turn
	Poor weight transfer at end of spin	Sink into boots, leaning shins against front cuff
Spinning out at end	Going too fast for spin stop	Don't use spin stop as a "fast stop"

T-stop

Problem	Reason	Correction
Spinning instead of stopping	Skate not dragging at 90 degrees	Practice T-position while stationary
		Flex weight more onto front skate
	Upper body not facing straight ahead	Check that hands are steady in Ready Position
	One or two wheels only dragging	Hold skate square to ground and feel all four wheels drag
Not stopping quickly	Not enough resistance applied to dragging wheels	Dig dragging skate gradually into ground

Take care that your weight is not too far forward when you are skating backward. If it is, you may trip over your toes.

Backward Skating

Problem	Reason	Correction
Unable to create any backward motion	Not swizzling backward properly	Revise forward swizzles
		Check reverse V-position
		Bend and extend away properly, pushing from toes
		Perform half-swizzle while stationary, with unweighted leg on either side
Unable to maintain backward motion	Not transferring weight fluidly or properly	Create a rhythm, saying out loud: "One, two; one, two," etc.
	Over-edging, creating resistance	Let wheels glide between each swizzle stroke

Backward Crossover

See the Troubles section on the forward crossover for basic problems, because they can occur whether you are traveling forward or backward.

Problem	Reason	Correction
Having to turn around to maintain balance	Not landing wheels in line with the angle of direction of travel	Ride each stride for longer and slow down a little
		Concentrate more on position and place each skate precisely
Traveling too fast, leading to loss of confidence	Shoulders too square and not looking over your shoulder	Stretch out your arms towards and focus on the direction of travel

05   Skillful Techniques

By now, your skating techniques simply need to be polished here and there while you learn a few expert moves, stops, and tricks. You will have mastered balance almost completely now, not just from the miles of skating experience under your feet, but also from the conscious and subconscious repetition of the moves that have become part of your natural repertoire. Now, it is a question of "What more is there to learn?" rather than "How am I going to do that?"

Power Striding

You can make your dynamic stride 25 percent more efficient, by refining it to become the power stride. This movement is well known to racing skaters, who strive to gain maximum speed while using minimum energy. It is not particularly difficult, but it does require the precise application of the edge to create maximum efficiency. Performed properly, it will increase your speed with only 75 percent of the effort.

Instead of beginning each stride from your center edges and finishing on your inner edges, begin from your outer edges. In each stride forward, you will roll from the outer, through the center, to the inner edge. The roll from the outside requires no extra effort, only the concentration to make the specific edge adjustment. From this point, simply stride normally. The effective use of energy should come quite naturally.

Look at the sequence for your position at the start of each stride. Your knee should lean out, with the skate under your body. This can be an unstable position, and without proper support from your other leg it will result in catching, skipping you and the skate sideways to regain balance.

1 *Land your skate on the outer edge in each stride.*

2 *Drive sideways and execute a normal stride.*

3 *As soon as you have completed one stride, land the other skate exactly on the outer edge.*

When you execute the power stride you must lean your knee outward to locate the outer edge at the beginning of each stride.

The sequence for power striding is:

1 **Outer edge**
2 **Stride**
3 **Outer edge**

Practice standing on the outer edges of both skates so that you know what it should feel like before you are in motion.

With the striding leg ready on the outer edge (1), and the other skate ready, drive sideways and execute a normal stride (2). As soon as you have completed one Stride, land the next skate precisely on its outer edge (3), at the same time transferring your weight and moving directly into a new stride. Continue to link the power strides together, and you should immediately notice a benefit from the extra power.

Repeat the sequence of steps in your head as you perform the move. Make sure that you are balanced at the critical moment when you first land the skate.

4 *At the same time, transfer your weight to the other leg and move directly into the next stride.*

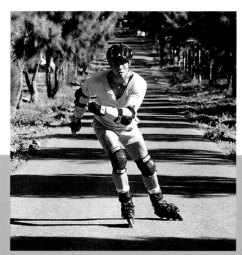

5 *Continue to link the strides together.*

Power Stopping

Hockey Stop

The hockey stop is probably one of the most effective stopping techniques. It is fast and dynamic, and it does not wear the wheels as heavily as the power slide (pages 86–87) does. It can, however, take a great deal of practice to get right.

Basically, the hockey stop is a very sharp, extreme parallel turn. It should not, however, to be confused with a lunge turn. The essence of a hockey stop is to drive the knees and ankles, combined with steering from your feet (especially your outside skate), very precisely and aggressively into a short, sharp arc.

The maneuver requires a great deal of balance and leg strength, because the forces can easily spin you out as you drive around. A common mistake is to fail to concentrate on the action at leg and skate level, but to throw the hips and body around wildly, which results in a clumsy and unattractive execution.

The sequence for performing a hockey stop is:

1   **Sink**
2   **Steer**
3   **Arc**

From a moderate glide, begin to prepare yourself by making a few linked slalom turns. Once you decide on your

1   *Once you have decided on your final turn, speed into it, driving your knees and ankles and steering your skates sharply into the turn.*

2   *Allow your legs to drift apart as you go into the turn.*

final turn, speed into it, driving the knees and ankles. Sink (1) into your boots as you steer (2) the edges and feet into a sharp arc (3). Concentrate your weight on the outer skate to keep the forces to the outside of the turn. This combined action should bring you to an abrupt stop.

It is important to keep your weight forward, with your hips over the balls of your feet, to prevent falling backward. Sudden hockey stops at speed will undoubtedly spin you out, so always slow down with a few sharp parallel turns beforehand.

Work on parallel turns to master this one, and refer to Skillful Techniques Troubles if you are having any problems.

3 *Concentrate your weight on the outer skate, and turn so that your upper body faces outward.*

4 *Drive down, so that your weight is on the edge of the outer skate. This will bring you to a stop.*

Power Slide

The pinnacle of in-line skating maneuvers, and commonly practiced as a "trick skill," the power slide is impressive but has no real practical use. There's no skipping it, however. Everyone learns to do the power slide! On the street, you'll always be seen as an intermediate skater until you can do it. So get ready to join the league of the advanced.

The way to approach learning this maneuver is to follow the method as closely as you can, and then to improve it through trial and error if you don't grasp the technique immediately. The power slide is the one move that catches everyone out! The reason the power slide is so difficult is that you will want to let the wheels of one skate slide in a controlled sideways slip. The friction of the wheels against the ground as they slide will bring you to a very abrupt stop. When approached properly, and with a strong commitment, it is actually quite simple.

The following method is the easiest approach to the power slide. Once you have performed it several times and learned how to slide the wheels of the skate, you will probably choose a faster method. Before you attempt the real thing, adopt the finish position shown [below] so you know what is expected.

The sequence for performing a Power Slide is:

1   **A-frame**
2   **Lunge**
3   **Stretch**

From a moderate-to-fast glide, open your legs into an A-frame (1), spreading them until they reach the widest, but most comfortable, position. Now begin to move as if you are making a lunge turn (2), keeping all your weight on your rear leg. However, don't actually turn; instead, pivot on your rear leg. At the same time, describe an arc around a rolling lead skate, letting it stretch dramatically (3) away from you. This

1 *From a moderate-to-fast glide, open your legs until they are as wide as is comfortable and you are in the A-frame position.*

2 *Turn as if you were about to start a lunge turn, keeping all your weight on your rear leg.*

3 *Do not turn, but pivot on your rear leg, at the same time rolling the wheels around in an arc.*

*It looks great,
but the
power slide
will wear out
your wheels.*

action should release the wheel edges and send them sliding sideways. There will be little or no weight on your lead leg as it comes around. When it is performed properly, your final position will feel like you are doing a hamstring stretch. The lead skate will also finish angled at approximately 90 degrees to the shadow skate.

Some methods of performing the power slide involve lifting the skate and "placing" it down on the sides of the wheels to initiate the slide. However, this is difficult and not very smooth. Don't be surprised if you see several versions of the power slide.

The disadvantage of using the power slide as a stopping technique is that it dramatically wears down the wheels. You will find using the hockey stop is much less abrasive and is more effective.

Remember that the power slide is not really for your benefit – it's for everyone else's!

4   *Continue to let your lead skate stretch away from
you as you continue to lean inward. This action
will release the edges of the wheels and send
them sliding sideways.*

Troubles

A static shot of foot position for the power stride.

Power Stride

Problem	Reason	Correction
No increased stride efficiency	Beginning each stride on center instead of outer edge	Practice while stationary for better outer edge feeling
		Lean knee further outward and place hand on knee to position edge
Unstable in the outer edge starting position	No balance compensation for extreme edge position	Flex ankles more
Striding not smooth	Leg too straight at beginning of stride	Flex legs and ankles more

Power Slide

Problem	Reason	Correction
Unable to initiate Slide	A-frame too narrow	Open legs further
	Not enough weight on rear leg	Lunge more onto rear leg
		Flex more into rear boot
		Straighten lead leg as you lean
	Not stretching lead leg away	Practice finish position while stationary

It is important to practice regularly all techniques needed to perform the various steps.

Hockey Stop

Problem	Reason	Correction
Stop not occurring	Throwing body into turn	Revise parallel turn to speed up arc
	Not sinking down and steering legs or feet	Place hands on thighs or knees and steer
Catching skates sideways	Trying to slide (skid) skates	While stationary, wheel roll sharp arc by rotating outside leg from hip
	Leaning too far into turn	Don't "follow" shoulders around too much
	Inner edges set at too extreme an angle	Practice guiding edges with hands on knees
Falling backward	Body not keeping up with speed of turn	Keep hips over ankles in turn; hold hands forward

Remember to use your arms to gather momentum when striding.

06   The Real World

Roads will not always be empty for your sole pleasure.
Photograph © Jack Gescheidt.

You may find skating on flat, smooth surfaces easy, but hills and rough terrain may deter you from considering long-distance journeys. You should put your techniques to the test, however. Leave the parking lot, park, or cycleway, and take up the challenge of rough and smooth, up and down. Seek adventure and excitement on country streets or in the chaos of urban city life.

Remember, however, that because you can go almost anywhere when you are in-line skating, it doesn't mean you're impervious to danger. As an in-line skater, you're both a pedestrian and a "vehicle," and this dual identity can be double trouble in the real world.

IISA Rules of the Road

The International In-Line Skating Association (IISA) has taken the lead in promoting in-line skating safety, and has issued some Rules of the Road as part of its safety campaign.

1. Skate smart

➜ Always wear your protective gear (helmet, wrist protections, elbow, and knee pads)

➜ Master the basic techniques (striding, stopping, and turning)

➜ Keep your equipment in good condition and proper working order

2. Skate alert

➜ Skate within your capabilities at all times

➜ Watch for street hazards

➜ Avoid skating through water, oil, sand, and grit

➜ Avoid traffic

3. Skate legal

➜ Obey all traffic regulations: when you are on skates you have the same obligations as any wheeled vehicle

4. Skate courteous

➜ Skate on the right, pass on the left

➜ Announce your intentions by saying, "Passing on your left"

➜ Always yield to pedestrians

Coping with Traffic

Skating in heavy traffic is not recommended. Weaving in and out of busy, bumper-to-bumper lines of cars poses obvious dangers, while skating single- or multi-lane highways is an absolute no, whether it is legal or not. As far as this book is concerned, skating traffic amounts to no more than slow-moving vehicles on streets where there is plenty of space for them to pass, and where there is space for you to retreat easily and safely. By day and night, always wear brightly colored or luminous clothing.

Always use hand signals when you change directions, as you would if you were on a bicycle, and give drivers plenty of notice of your intentions. Don't make sudden changes in direction. Keep an eye on the drivers of vehicles, try to predict their route, and anticipate their mistakes. Be courteous and give in-line skating a good name.

Pedestrians and Skating Sidewalks

Always give pedestrians right of way. They will be moving more slowly than you, so give them plenty of room as you pass. Don't expect to step off the curb into the street or onto the grass to let you through; if they do, always thank them. If you are approaching someone from behind, call out to indicate on which side you intend to pass. It is easy to startle someone . Always keep to this rule. In-line skaters are responsible and friendly!

Take special care when you are approaching blind street entrances and driveways: these can be lethal! Always check your speed, and stop if necessary, even if you hear no traffic. Be safe, and never assume that nothing is coming. Always anticipate that there will be traffic or pedestrians.

Don't skate close around corners either. You could easily meet a pedestrian and crash into them. Senior citizens, the physically challenged, young children, and dogs should also be given extra room. Their movements are likely to be less predictable, and they are most likely not to see you coming.

Always remember that an in-line skater wearing protective gear can be an intimidating sight.

Whenever possible, signal or indicate your intentions to pedestrians.

Street Skating

Finding roads without traffic provides excellent opportunities for speed skating.

Going street skating is not like taking a stride in the park or a whiz around a parking lot with your personal stereo blaring in your ears. Street skating is potentially very dangerous and requires a fail-safe technique, a high degree of awareness, and lightning reactions. If you plan to skate in the street, near traffic, or among pedestrians, think of yourself as a porcelain ornament on a stock-car track. Protective gear, including a helmet, is essential. Also, remember that in-line skating is a relatively new pastime, other people on the street won't be expecting you and won't know how to predict or anticipate your movements. This can make them nervous and irritable. You are the underdog, but don't expect any sympathy if you make a mistake. Behave like an angel, but skate like a demon. That way, you'll reap the rewards that accompany the challenge and enjoyment of sharing the millions of miles of asphalt designed primarily for the automobile.

Skating off a curb is easy. Check for traffic and prepare for a possible change of speed if the surface looks different. Keep your weight low, flexing your knees and ankles well. Push your hands forward as you step down, and transfer you weight precisely. On difficult surfaces or an undulating pavement, scissoring your skates will spread your weight over a greater area and give you more stability. Make use of the scissor often.

One essential check to make is whether it is legal for you to skate on the streets and sidewalks of your locality since, sometimes, laws have been passed preventing it. You can find out from your local police department.

Traffic is, of course, the greatest danger. However, skating over changing surfaces, jumping curbs, avoiding potholes, and negotiating trash cans and other obstacles will all add to your urban asphalt adventure.

Changing surfaces, stepping curbs, and avoiding potholes, trash cans, and other obstacles are all part of skating the streets.

The Real World   95

Uneven surfaces are best approached with well-flexed legs. The scissor is the best technique for crossing them.

Coping with Varying Surfaces

For some, a smooth surface may be a luxury; others may take it for granted. Wherever you skate there will be times when you encounter varying asphalt surfaces. You may see them coming, or you may not. In some cases, the asphalt may be so rough that it is impossible to skate. In general, however, only loose gravel or severe undulations in the pavement will stop the wheels completely. Stretches of poor surface are best crossed at speed, as long as that does not increase the dangers significantly. If you are traveling too slowly, you will feel all the lumps and bumps, but if you skim them quickly, the experience won't be so uncomfortable.

To move from one surface to another and stay balanced, scissor your skates for maximum stability and to reduce the risk of falling or being caught out. You should learn to use the scissor regularly.

Sand, gravel, and water should always be avoided. Sand will not only slow you down, but it will also get into

the bearings, causing such severe damage that they will need a complete overhaul. If left, it may cause them to seize up completely.

Gravel will cause obvious problems. Apart from fine gravel getting into the bearings, larger stones can get trapped in the wheels, causing them to jam and trip you up. If you have to cross an area of gravel, skate at walking speed or, better still, step it.

Skating in the rain or on wet surfaces is dangerous. If the asphalt is greasy, which is often the case when it rains after a long dry spell, skating is virtually impossible. In these circumstances do not even attempt to slalom turn downhill. You will slip and fall. Even if your wheels appear to maintain grip on a wet surface, the water will act in the same way as sand and cause serious corrosion to the bearings. These are not completely sealed, so look after them and don't skate in the rain.

Gravel can cause the wheels of your skates to jam, and this can be dangerous, so avoid crossing areas of gravel if at all possible.

Begin to develop downhill control by practicing on a gentle slope. Hold your skates in "snow plough" position, with your toes pointing in and your heels apart. From there, apply the techniques learned in the A-frame, "swinging to the hill" with each turn.

Basic Hill Techniques

Hills may appear to be a daunting challenge in skating, which is not an action normally associated with them. The traditional images of ice skating or quad roller-skating do not involve hills. They do feature in in-line skating, however, but the method for dealing with them is more akin to snow skiing than skating. If the hill is so steep that the action of skating isn't required to generate momentum, in practice you are no longer skating but skiing.

Basic Control Downhill

The most obvious and easiest way to learn to control speed downhill is to begin on a gentle incline, before progressing to increasingly steeper challenges. There are three principal methods of controlling speed downhill: using the heel brake; braking by means of a gradual T-stop; and slalom turning.

Using the heel brake is a common method of controlling speed downhill, and it is used by novices and experts alike. It is a fail-safe technique that comes into play at all stages of the descent. Continuous use of the heel brake, of course, means continuous wear. However, this is a small price to pay

for going where you want if you have not yet perfected any of the other hill techniques.

In the T-stop, the wheels provide the resistance necessary for speed control. Anyone who has removed the heel brake to allow trick and aggressive skating will know how important it is to learn to T-brake. Again, however, the price is increased wheel wear, which is expensive. The heel brake is a better option in terms of replacement costs.

When you are traveling downhill, wheels suffer the least wear when slalom turning is employed. Controlling your speed with this technique is similar to a skiing action, and involves the precise steering and edge control of a good parallel turn, a technique that snow skiers strive for. To slow down using the slalom turn technique, you must understand that each turn is actually an arc back up the hill. In skiing, this is known as a "swing to the hill," and this fact will determine whether you are slowing down in each turn or accelerating into it. The slalom turn can cause both situations, but usually the latter if the difference between them is not known or fully understood. Mastering the slalom turn as a slowing technique requires gradually learning edge feel, pressure control, and foot and leg steering.

Skating Uphill

The fun and speed of skating downhill is countered by the positive workout you will experience when traveling uphill. Muscle power and good skating rhythm are needed for an easy ascent, and this is where the real energy is spent. The fitness benefits are immediate. Maintaining a steady striding pace will keep the wheels rolling. Do not allow them to slip at the end of each stroke, but keep the momentum going. It will feel difficult to begin with, but once you have established a rhythm, the task will be easier.

The wheels of your skates should land across the hill, so that they do not slip at the end of each stroke. Turn your feet out, driving sideways and projecting your body upward and forward with each stride. Use your hands and arms to help maintain your momentum.

You can skate up most hills, but consider the surface and the angle of the slope to determine its Gliding potential and its relative ease. Skating uphill is the activity that will require the greatest energy, so read the fitness programs overleaf.

The wheels should land across the hill so that they do not slip as you finish each step. Turn your feet out, driving sideways and projecting your body upward and forward with each stride. Use your arms and hands to help you maintain the forward momentum.

Skating for Fitness

In-line skating is a great way to get fit. It doesn't seem as if you're working out on skates, because everything is so much fun. The sport has proved to be beneficial for both lungs and muscle tone. It also scores well because it is a low-impact sport, unlike, say, running, which can be little more than the rather laborious pounding of never-ending streets.

On your in-line skates you won't experience the intimidation that many people complain of when they go to a gym or an expensive health club. While keep-fit fanatics are confined to four walls, using the treadmill, exercise bike, and rowing machine, the in-line skater is burning up calories while breathing in fresh air and is constantly surrounded by ever-changing scenery.

Studies have also shown that in-line skating is a better all-round workout than running or cycling. Although running is actually a more aerobic activity than skating, it doesn't develop the leg muscles (especially the quads and hamstring muscles) nearly as much.

In-line skating is a great rehabilitation activity, too. Anyone who has suffered the ever-increasing risk of injury to their knees through continuous impact exercise, will be pleased to know that in-line skating significantly strengthens the muscles above the knees (the vastus medialis) without damaging them in the process. In addition, it greatly improves posture: the abdominals, obliques and spinal muscles of the torso work together to keep the upper body erect. In fact, all of the following muscle areas greatly benefit from in-line skating:

Thighs (quadriceps)

Buttocks (gluteals)

Stomach (abdominals)

Chest (pectorals)

During a 30-minute period, at a steady comfortable rate, an in-line skater expends 285 calories and produces a heart rate of 148 beats a minute. Interval skating – that is, combining periods of all-out sprinting with periods of slower skating – expends 450 calories in the same time. Running and cycling expend 350 and 360 calories respectively at a heart rate of 148 beats a minute.

The faster you go, the more energy you burn!
Everyday recreational skating will maintain and improve your fitness levels, provided you skate for at least 20 minutes and generate a sweat. However, because you are reading this chapter, no doubt you want to make a significant improvement to your fitness through in-line skating, and probably want a longer schedule to stick to.

The following program has been supplied by Rollerblade® and is called the 30 Minute Workout™.

1　*Skate for five minutes at a slow, warm-up speed.*
2　*Increase speed to a steady workout pace for 20 minutes.*
3　*Decrease speed to a cool-down pace for the last five minutes of skating.*
4　*Complete the workout with a few cool-down stretches.*

This workout, performed three or four times a week for three months, can increase aerobic capacity by 15-20 percent and burn approximately 14,000 calories. As the skater's physical condition improves, the workout can be intensified by skating faster or by increasing the workout time.

As an alternative, you could try the Rollerblade® 30 Minute Interval Workout™.

1　*Skate for five minutes at a slow, warm-up speed.*
2　*For the next 20 minutes, alternate 1 minute of all-out sprint skating in a tucked racing position with 1 minute of easy skating in an upright position.*
3　*Cool down with five minutes of easy skating.*
4　*Finish with cool-down stretching.*

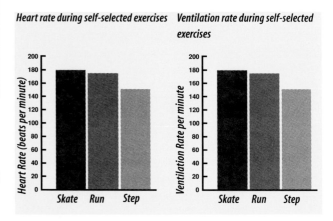

Heart rate during self-selected exercises　　**Ventilation rate during self-selected exercises**

Take time out betweeen heavy exercise routines.

Skating in groups can offer healthy competition and encouragement for improving your skills.
Photograph: Stockfile/ Steven Behr.

This interval workout can burn about 20,000 calories when it is performed three or four times a week for three months. Because you will be traveling faster, you will expend more energy and, once again, your physical condition will improve.

High-intensity programs can be designed based on these simple workouts by extending the period. The possibilities for devising your own workout schemes are endless, but to benefit properly from an all-round workout on skates, it is important to vary your stride, direction, and even the surfaces you skate on. Crossover training in a circle is probably the quickest and easiest way to work up a sweat. The muscular power and skill required to maintain a constant pace is higher than if you travel the same distance in a straight line.

Visit your local fitness center or contact your local in-line skating club to discover other ways in which you can use your skates for fitness.

Skate to Ski

Controlling speed downhill is normally a matter of applying one of the methods covered in Basic Hill Techniques on pages 98-99, but there is such a close similarity between snow-skiing techniques and slalom turning downhill that to improve and maintain good style and control on the descent it is necessary to think "skiing." This section is for skaters who want to develop their downhill technique and for skiers who want to use in-line skates to brush up their skiing technique between snow seasons.

The fundamental difference between skiing and skating is that on skis you can skid, but on skates you cannot. A skier, therefore, must quickly learn to apply the technique necessary for carve turning, a skill that is often difficult to grasp on snow, yet is far more easily applied and understood on skates. Simulating carved turns on skates can give the intermediate skier the sensation of the perfect carved turn, so it is unbeatable training for performing the technique on snow.

 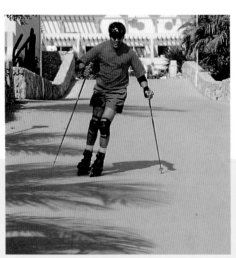 

1 *Each turn steers the skates perfectly into a carved "swing to the hill." From the end of the turn, the pole is planted to provide support and to help initiate the next turn.*

2 *Let the skates move more quickly for no more than a second as they travel downhill in the middle of a turn.*

3 *Drive your knees and steer with your feet into the direction of the turn in order to slow down.*

Downhill, the narrower, shorter platform of the skate also provides a greater test of balance than the longer, wider ski. This makes perfecting the ski turn on skates a truer test of a skier's balance and posture. Expert skiers know that their weight should be balanced perfectly over their feet, but a good technique can compensate for their weight being too far forward or back. On in-line skates, however, if the weight shifts backward or forward, there is no disguising it, and the result is normally a fall.

Practicing ski technique when skating downhill, with ski poles for balance and timing, is excellent training. Of course, if you are not a skier, trying to understand how and when to use ski poles may only add to your problems. Choose a gentle, smooth slope with no obstacles for your early attempts at skiing on skates. A good skiing technique requires the hands to be apart. Do not rotate your upper body as you turn. The turn is initiated by the legs and feet – your shoulders should continue to face downhill.

4 *Maintain balance by keeping the arms steady in preparation for the next turn. Precise concentration is essential.*

5 *The extra movement should allow you to relax your arms and swing them from side to side across your body. Keep your left arm straight when your left leg is straight and vice versa.*

First Tricks

Tricks can be learned at any time. They are not just impressive exhibitions of skill, but are a good test of balance and will help further develop your all-round skating abilities.

Toe/Heel

This maneuver involves balancing on two wheels only – no. 1 of your rear skate and no. 4 of your front skate in a scissor position. Lifting onto no. 4 shouldn't be so difficult, but balancing on no. 1 requires the ballet technique of pointing your toes. Don't move too quickly into this. It is best to begin from a slow glide.

360-degree Spin or Pirouette

Begin from a slow glide and stretch out your arms level with your shoulders so that you can use them to help you initiate a spin. Rotate your shoulders and bring in your arms to begin the spin. At the same time place your skates in a V-position, steering with your feet as you go round. As you turn, be aware of the way your balance shifts, and transfer your weight from one leg to the other to maintain your balance.

The toe/heel involves standing on no. 1 wheel of your rear skate and no. 4 wheel of your front skate.

The cartwheel on skates is comparatively straightforward but requires gymnastic skills.

Two Toes

This is like the toe/heel, except that you must balance on the no. 1 wheel of each skate. The action requires precise balance and produces acute pressure on the tips of your toes as they support your weight. Practice the position on grass, holding onto something for balance, before you attempt to do it on the move.

Reverse Snake

Begin with a backward glide, then stretch out one leg behind you. Keep your leg straight and raise your foot until the skate is resting on the no. 1 wheel. You should be balancing on your front leg while you complete this maneuver. Continue to Glide backward and "snake" along, moving the skate from one side to the other in a "weaving" motion. This is a good trick to practice to improve your balancing skills.

1 *360-degree spin. From a slow glide, hold out your arms straight at either side.*

2 *Rotate your shoulders, bring in your arms and begin to spin, making sure your skates are in the V-position. Steer with your feet as you turn.*

3 *Redistribute your weight as you turn, timing the shift from one leg to the other to maintain your balance.*

Hockey

One of the fastest-growing applications of in-line skating is hockey. This hugely popular sport combines all the benefits of in-line skating with added thrills, exhilaration, camaraderie, and teamwork.

The skills of skating at speed, turning, stopping, dodging, and weaving are combined with the skills of controlling a hockey stick and puck – dribbling, passing, receiving, taking evasive action, and even scoring a goal. It's all happening at once, and it's all happening on skates.

Playing in-line hockey is the single quickest way to learn how to control your skates. You will naturally adopt a balanced position, and react to the changing direction and speed with more instinct than thought. With no deliberate checking allowed in most in-line hockey the sport is relatively injury-free and will prove the greatest teaching aid for all-round control.

Casual games, where no formal hockey skills are required, are common and skaters can often be found playing on parking lots or basketball courts and welcome new players. This is "pick-up" hockey can be joined at will.

As soon as you are relatively competent with stopping and turning, there are really only two other basic skills to learn: stick handling and puck/ball control. This is the most accessible hockey in terms of understanding the game and it will give you the basic skills and disciplines to prepare you for competitive, organized hockey.

Mandatory Equipment

Some protective playing equipment is mandatory. Players under the age of 18 must wear:

> **Helmet designed for hockey**
> **Full-face shield designed for hockey**
> **Internal mouth guard**
> **Elbow pads**
> **Gloves**
> **Knee and shin protection**
> **Protective abdominal cup (males)**

Players over the age of 18 must also wear all of the above equipment with the exception of a full-face shield. However, a full- or half-face shield is strongly recommended.

Skates

In-line skates intended for hockey need to be tougher and a little heavier than those used for speed racing or recreational skating in order to increase durability. All mainstream skate manufacturers produce skates designed specifically for in-line hockey, though it is possible to temporarily convert skates into another type simply by fitting the correct sport-specific wheels.

Wheels

Specific in-line hockey wheels are designed to withstand the constant high-speed changes of direction performed during games. The sizes, profiles, and hardness (durometer) of hockey wheels vary according to the surface to be skated on and your preference. Hockey is prone to eat wheels, so rotate the position of your wheels on the frame frequently.

Frames

The frame that contains the wheels deserves serious attention. There are frames that are part of factory assembled in-line skates and there are hockey frames that can be purchased separately, possibly as an upgrade. A new vibrant and competitive market has recently emerged as a result of downsizing in the Californian aerospace industry and the abundant supply of skilled technicians.

The majority of frames still take four wheels, but they can also take five. The logic is that while smaller wheels are slower, a frame with five wheels lowers your center of gravity thus providing greater maneuverability and stability.

So what's on offer? You pays your money, and you gets your choice! Spending more generally gets you better aluminum combined with better design and more costly production processes. The more expensive frames provide greater torsion strength and are less susceptible to bending. The best frame delivers maximum strength and maneuverability with minimal weight.

Also, check to see if the chassis is versatile. Does it offer various front-to-back wheel placements and rockering options? In the store, ask for a demonstration to see how instinctive and quick the axle system is.

When buying equipment generally, do your research by checking the products of a range of different manufacturers, check the various published equipment guides in the magazines like *Inline Hockey News* and *Roller Hockey*. Talk to independent dealers and your friends.

Where to Play

In-line hockey can be played outdoors on parking lots, roller rinks, basketball courts, and on other open flat surfaces. Or it can be played indoors in purpose-built facilities.

Who to Contact

There are two magazines that are widely available on the newsstands that both have league and club listings state by state. They are: *Inline Hockey News* and *Roller Hockey* magazine.

Alternatively, there are two main in-line hockey organisations which both offer comprehensive membership packages with a range of useful benefits. Both associations offer insurance programs and access to a wide range of leagues and tournaments for different age groups. Contact either organisation for further details (information listed at the back of the book).

Basic Hockey Rules

→ Rink size: The most common size is 180' long by 90' wide and could be outdoor or indoor, permanent, or temporary. All official rinks are surrounded by some sort of board structure to contain the puck or ball.

→ Teams: Teams usually consist of four players on the rink plus one goalkeeper. The maximum permissible number of players on a team roster is 14 including goalkeepers.

→ Goal size: The most widely used goal cage is 6' across by 4' high, but some rules specify cages of 67" by 42".

→ Time periods: The length of a game varies according to the rules you play under. Games of 2 by 15 minute periods, or 4 quarters of 12 minutes are both common and both have intervals after each period.

→ Starting play: Play always starts with a face-off from the center spot on the halfway line.

→ Body-checking: There's no deliberate body checking in in-line hockey, though unintentional contact is tolerated.

→ Fighting: Most leagues operate a zero tolerance rule which forbids fighting.

→ Off-side: Some leagues operate a center line off-side, some don't in order to allow players to move more freely around the tink and accept breakaway passes from team-mates.

A hockey helmet is very durable and should be worn with a full face guard.

Equipment

Although you do not need any specialized equipment to play pick-up hockey, if you plan to play a lot or if you want to play competitive in-line hockey, you will need some special stitched leater or reinforced nylon hockey boots, which will provide greater support for your feet and ankles than standard recreational boots.

If you play a lot of hockey, you will need skates with stiffer than normal frames. Hockey also wears wheels quickly, and it is possible to obtain special wheels that are designed to withstand the constant high-speed changes of direction. These wheels are normally smaller, but wider, than standard.

Players of full body contact hockey should wear fully padded clothing to proect them from being hit by a high-speed ball or puck. Goal-keepers need to be protected from head to foot, because they are even more likely to be hit by a flying puck or ball.

A variety of sticks and pucks are available from stores that specialize in in-line skates. A ball is usually used for outdoor games played on uneven surfaces, where it can travel fast and be difficult to control. The better-quality equipment will last for longer, although it is, of course, more expensive.

Hockey girdle. This is just one of the items that is mandatory for full contact hockey. Others include shoulder pads, gloves, and shin pads.

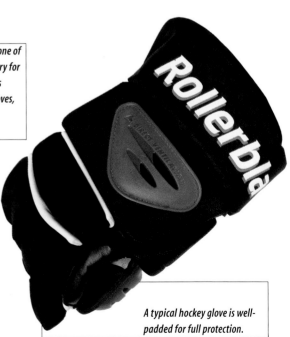

A typical hockey glove is well-padded for full protection.

Melzen NHL home teamshirt

A hockey stick should reach the top of your chin for size.

Pucks and balls are available in many different versions. Some allow air to pass through and glide smoothly and easily.

Cesar Mora, one
of the leading
U.S. Vert
champions.
Photograph
© *Jack Gescheidt.*

Aggressive Skating

Aggressive skating, which used to be known as extreme skating, has gained an enormous following, and it is now achieving even greater popularity through the exposure it has received in the media reporting of both national and international competitions.

Skate parks are havens for aggressive skaters, who are often pictured in the media throwing big air in the half-pipe. There are no limits on aggressive skating, which ranges from skating the street, to skating the rail – anything goes, and it often involves a degree of danger.

**A toe grab in full
flight.**
*Photography cour-
tesy K2.*

Ramp-riding is really popular. Check out this handstand on the ramp's rail.

Half-pipe

The "king" of the half-pipe or Vert skating has long been Chris Edwards, who pioneered the sport in the mid- and late 1980s, and promoted it through videos, magazines, and television. He is so well known that a skate has been named after him. He has inspired dozens of young skaters, who perform heart-stopping tricks in the air, including the Heel or Toe Grab, or the Mute Fakey.

This is easily the most impressive form of skating for the viewer, but skaters who attempt the half-pipe and similar feats must wear full protective gear to protect them from the knocks they receive on landing and to provide the support they need on take-off.

NISS Competition, Venice Beach, California.
Photograph:
Stockfile/
Steven Behr.

NISS Competition, Venice Beach, California.
Photograph
© Jack Gescheidt.

Aggressive Skating Gear

Grinding plates are available separately for standard frames and can be fitted easily.

Extreme knee pads. They are larger and tougher than regular pads.

Aggressive skates have smaller wheels, are very robust, and a metal reinforced frame for grinding.

Grinding
Photography
courtesy K₂.

Street Skating

Enthusiasts of this kind of skating choose areas where there are obstacles to jump off and over, and where they can practice wall riding and "rail riding" or "grinding." Grinding is the popular but hazardous activity of jumping onto handrails and sliding down them. Various tricks and techniques are performed as the skater descends the rails. These involve a high degree of risk for learners, and full protective gear is essential.

Stair riding is another technique enjoyed by street skaters. If you want to try this, choose comfortably spaced steps with a gentle incline. Scissor the skates and, keeping your weight low over the center of both skates, relax as you descend. Take care that you do not lean too far forward, and do not catch the brake on the edge of a step. Street skaters often remove the brake for this kind of maneuver.

The equipment used for aggressive skating must be both durable and robust. The skates must be comfortable but strong. Wheels are small and designed to execute tight turns, with a low center of gravity. Some skates are specially designed for grinding, and these have "grind plates," which are built-in metal protectors for the frame. Grind plates can be bought separately to protect standard frames, and they are essential if grinding is practiced regularly.

Stair riding

*Stair riding forwards or backwards –
a similar technique is required both
ways.*

Racing attracts hundreds of competitors as seen at the New York Champs.
All photographs © Jack Gescheidt.

Lone racer.
Photograph courtesy K₂.

Racing

Racing or speed skating was the first form of in-line skating to be organized at a competitive level, and its success has been responsible for the technical development in many other aspects of the sport, setting new standards for both equipment and techniques.

Racing offers its supporters a combination of the thrill of speed, endurance, and the satisfaction of competing at the highest physical level. The distances covered range from short-track of half a mile to long-distance, endurance races.

It is smooth, fast, and the closest thing to flying in in-line skating, but it does need the right equipment. Although it is possible to compete if you have standard four-wheel recreational skates, the really top speeds are achieved on five-wheel skates. These specially designed skates have low cuffs and, usually, leather boots. Most serious racers choose to build their own skates from the speed equipment that is now available, choosing custom-fit boots, frames that are specifically designed for particular stroke patterns, and faster wheels and bearings.

Regular training, good technique, and the right equipment are the keys to success in racing. The aerodynamics are also important, and experienced racers usually wear tight-fitting Lycra® suits and do without elbow and knee pads, which cause wind drag. Gloves are preferred to wrist guards, but helmets are mandatory. Most race organizers will not allow you to compete if you are not wearing a helmet.

The techniques required to maintain speed and stamina over the long distances that are involved in high-speed racing include starting, effective stroking, good posture, and pacing. Some in-line skating clubs run special programs and can advise on how to get started and how to enter races. At first, however, you should look out for the recreational, fun races that are organized around the country. Try one of these to get a taste for the sport before moving onto the real thing.

Useful Addresses

Contact the following governing bodies and organizations for further information:

U.S.A.

International In-line Skating Association (IISA)
3720 Farragut Avenue
Suite 400
Kensington
Maryland 20895
USA
Telephone: 310 942 9770

National In-Line Hockey Association (NIHA)
999 Brickell Avenue
9th Floor
Miami
Florida
USA
e-mail: NIHAMIAMI@aol.com

United States Amateur Confederation of Roller Skating
4730 South St.
P.O. Box 6579
Lincoln
Nebraska, 68506
USA

USA Hockey InLine
4965 North 30th Street
Colorado Springs, CO 80919
USA

Aggressive Skaters Association
171 Pier Avenue
Suite 247
Santa Monica, CA 90405
USA

CANADA

NIHA (Canada)
11810 Kingsway
Edmonton, AB T5G 0X5
Canada

The Canadian In-Line & Roller Skating Association
679 Queens Quay West
Unit 117
Toronto
Ontario M5V 3A9
Canada

UNITED KINGDOM

British In-Line Skating Association (BISA)
Suite 479
2 Old Brompton Road
London SW7 3DQ
Telephone: 0976 271 699
Fax: 0171 581 445

British In-Line Puck Hockey Association (BIPHA)
140 Radstock Road
Woolston
Southampton
Hants SO2 7HU
Telephone: 01703 398712

Southern Rink Hockey Association
39 Old Magazine Close
Marchwood
Southampton
Hants SO40 4SD
Telephone: 01703 860030
Contact: P. S. Mence

British Skater Hockey Association
Grammont
Chiddingly Road
Horam
Heathfield
East Sussex TN21 0JH

Previous page:
Photograph
© Jack Gescheidt

Useful Internet In-line Site
SKATING THE INFOBAHN
http://www/skatecity.com/In
dex
Information on where, how,
why and what in the world of
in-line skating.

Glossary

A-frame Term used to describe the shape the body adopts when the feet are spread apart.

ABEC Internationally recognized standards set by the Annular Bearing Engineering Council for assessing the quality of bearings.

Aggressive skating The extreme end of in-line skating.

Allen wrench A tool used for removing wheel axles.

Asphalt A generic word used to describe street or pavement construction material suitable for skating.

Axle cap The nut to which the wheel axle is screwed.

Ball bearings Circular metal balls; the moving parts that enable the wheels to turn smoothly.

Bearing casing The donut-shaped container for the ball bearing.

Bearing lubricant Light oil specially made for lubricating ball bearings.

Bio-mechanical Designed to work efficiently with body movements.

Brake A pad, usually rubber, located at the rear of the skate.

Crossover A turn that crosses over skates while at the same time maintaining or increasing speed.

Duck walk An alternative name for V-walk.

Durometer The standard by which the hardness of wheels is measured.

Dynamic Ready Position Effectively balanced for action on the move.

Dynamic striding Explosive, more energetic striding.

Edges Inner, center, or outer position of the skate on its wheels.

Edging The action of specifically positioning the edges.

Elbow pads Plastic-covered protection for elbows.

Flexed The result of bending the joints.

Flexing Bending the joints.

Footbed The removable sole in-liner, designed for better fit and comfort.

Glide The free-rolling of skates.

Gluteals The muscles in the buttocks.

Grinding The skill of frame-sliding on rails.

Half-pipe A wooden or metal ramp designed to create airborne jumps.

Hamstring The tendon located at the back of the leg.

Helmet Vital protection against head injuries.

Hockey stop A fast and aggressive intermediate/advanced stopping technique.

In-line skates Skates with four or, occasionally, more wheels in a line.

Knee pads Plastic-covered protection for knees.

Lead foot/leg/skate The dominant foot, leg, or skate, which is determined by natural, instinctive use.

Liner The inner boot of the skate that lies next to the foot.

Multi-clip A buckle-closure system, used for fit and improved retention.

Mute Fakey A trick in Vert skating.

Non-ABEC A bearing that does not conform to ABEC standards.

Oblique A muscle in the stomach.

Polyamide A highly durable complex plastic.

Polymer A highly durable complex plastic.

Polyurethane A hard-waring plastic used in the construction of skates.

Power slide An advanced stopping technique.

Power striding The name given to the technique of dynamic striding.

Precision A term used to describe lower-quality, non-ABEC bearings.

Pressure The application of weight to the skate and wheels, resulting in a turn or other similar action.

Profile The thickness of the wheel.

Protection equipment/gear Clothing designed to protect the body from falls or from fast-moving hockey puck and ball.

Puck The rubber or plastic disc used for roller hockey.

Quads (1)The term often used for first-generation four-wheeled roller skates. (2) The muscles at the top of the legs.

Rails Banisters or poles for grinding.

Ramps Launch pads for air tricks; an alternative name for a half-pipe.

Ready Position The balanced starting position from which skating techniques are executed.

Recreational All-round skating or skates.

Reverse snake A simple backward trick.

Rockerable A skate on which the wheels can be lowered or raised.

Rockerers The small wheel pin locators that can be inverted in the frame to lower or raise the wheels.

Rockering The action of inverting rockers to lower or raise the wheels.

Rotating The switching of the position of wheels to prevent uneven wear.

Scissoring The positioning of one skate forward; used in many techniques to give greater stability.

Scoot Stroking one leg at a time; bringing the skate back to the center.

Semi-precision A term used to described poorer-quality, non-ABEC bearings.

Shadow foot/leg/skate The less dominant foot, leg, or skate.

Shell The exterior of the skate boot.

Skate Smart The IISA name for its code for safe skating.

Skate tool A handy, multi-use wrench or tool, used for adjustment and maintenance.

Slalom turn Linked parallel turns, often performed downhill.

Spacers Plastic hubs that separate bearing castings.

Spec Abbreviation for "specification".

Specialist skating Specific applications of in-line skating.

Street skating Urban skating, including jumping obstacles.

Stride An active combination of stroke and Glide.

Stroke The skating action of the leg that provides propulsion.

Swizzle A technique of steering and driving skates in an hourglass or lemon-shaped arc.

T-position The static position, with the heels together and toes pointing outward, in which the wheels are prevented from rolling.

Toe-slide A trick in grinding.

Toe-up A vital aspect of the heel-stop technique.

Upgrade The replacement of components with better quality items that improve the performance of skates.

Urethane A plastic used in the construction of skates and components.

V-position The basic position for skating or beginning other techniques.

V-walk A learning move in the progression to Stroking.

Vert skating Airborne skating in the half-pipe.

Wheel axle The bolt pin that locates the wheels and bearing.

Wheel frame A frame of nylon or another similar material underneath the shell in which the wheels are located.

Wrist guards Gloves designed to protect the wrists from injury.

Index

Acknowledgements

Thank you to the following organizations and contributors for their help with this book; it would not have been possible without them.

Rollerblade® In-Line Skates
International In-Line Skating Association (IISA)
First In-Line Magazine
Hyper Wheels
Road Runner, London

Sun and Snow, London
Skate Attack, London
Ski 47, London
Graeme Saxby Bsc (Hons)
Registered osteopath
(page 35)
Alistair Gordon (pages 106–107)
Dawn Irwin (pages 98–99)
Ben Roberts
IISA qualified instructions and demonstrators
Samantha Tuson Ford
BladeMarc

The Publisher would also like to thank the following for supplying photographs:
K2 Exotech In-Line Skates
P.O. Box 1
Broad Ground Road
Lakeside
Redditch
Worcs. B98 8NQ
(pages 8–9, 10, 11, 16(t), 16(b), 110(l), 117(t))

Lucy Buxton
(pages 106–107)

Stockfile
5 High Street
Sunningdale
Berkshire SL5 0LX
England
(pages 12(t), 13(b), 17(t), 17(b), 29(t), 99(b), 111(t))

Rollerblade® (page 14)

Jack Gescheidt/U.S.
Tel: 415 668 5225
(pages 13, 15(t), 92(t), 110(l), 111(b), 116(t), 116(c), 116(b), 117(b), 112–123)